Towards a
Real Rotterdam

Aaron Betsky

Essay 01

ARCHITECTURE BULLETIN N° 02|2006

Rotterdam is the paradigmatic modern city, not just in terms of its image of no-nonsense landscapes of containerized transhipment and gridded blocks that facilitate the movement of people or data, but also in the physical isolation this obsession with the movement of goods, people and data produces. Ironically, the city dedicated to flows is made up of isolated objects. It has been called a 'city of islands', and in many ways it is no more than a collection of well-designed storage facilities for people asleep, at work or at leisure, for goods, or for data, completely overwhelmed by a heroic architecture of movement. While the cranes and bridges mark Rotterdam's skyline, the rest of the city is a collection of beautifully designed but not very recognizable blocks.

The mutual separation of Rotterdam's various neighbourhoods, and of the whole southern part of the city from the north by the main axis of the largest harbour in Europe, is emulated in the lack of clear relationship between the major buildings and by a lack of liaison to the street. Rotterdam may be 'Manhattan on the Maas', but without New York's unifying grid, it has none of that city's delirious potential. The real task for this city is to develop a spatial arrangement that will give it urban cohesion and density.

The reason for this isolation is partly an accident of history and partly a result of conscious choices in the city's economic development. Like most of the larger urban agglomerations in the Western Netherlands, the city sits on a former swamp. Its core is, again like most of its sister cities, the highest part of the area – it was an island or sandbank

Aaron Betsky (1958) is director of the Cincinnati Art Museum in the United States, and publishes regularly on diverse aspects of visual culture. He was director of the Netherlands Architecture Institute from 2001 to 2006. Under his leadership during the last five and a half years, the NAI has produced eighty exhibitions, an extensive programme of lectures and other activities, and the first issue of Architecture Bulletin. Betsky has acquired an international profile as a warm proponent of Dutch architecture. During his period in the Netherlands, he developed a love for Rotterdam, a tough city full of unfulfilled promise.

where the River Rotte was dammed. Subsequent urban expansion, however, did not grow around this dam, as it did in Amsterdam or even Gouda, but were separate additions that answered particular needs at particular times. From the second half of the 19th century onward, the harbour colony of Delft, Delftshaven, the areas dedicated to various port activities along the river, from the places where grain and wheat from the North and East were unloaded to the passenger terminals, as well as the workers' colonies, were all added to the landscape by competing developers. Each had its own place, character, and formal characteristics. Even the Rose plan of 1855, which is as close as Rotterdam ever came to planning an incremental area to supplement its core through a concentric infrastructure, failed to have the kind of formal focal points that helped 'connect the dots' from the historic inner city to new areas of development in cities such as Amsterdam.

As the city developed mainly as a port, it also lost its monumental focus to what became a more and more isolated harbour area. While the original shipping area was close to the city's downtown, it moved to the southern side of the Maas in the middle of the 19th century and has been moving further west ever since. Now there is little shipping at all within a ten-kilometer radius of downtown. While this is economically and functionally logical, it deprives Rotterdam of a sense of being intertwined with the activity that gave it its character. The more recent development of a major east-west axis of road, rail and oil transit to the south of the harbour further isolates this economic livelihood from urban experience.

Though the inner-city harbours have been recycled, their design has only acted as a palimpsest of their formerly isolated development. Both the 'Kop van Zuid' and the 'Lloydkwartier' areas are developing as enclaves of luxury housing, culture, and some office activity that stand in strong contrast to, and in clear isolation from, the economically depressed areas they adjoin.

The simple reason for much of this isolation lies in the geography of the area and the way human beings have reacted to those conditions. More often than not, the isolation is the result of dikes that protect this exposed city from the sea and the Maas River, Meuse as well as from the inundations of

smaller rivers and creeks. These secondary dikes are an omnipresent part of Rotterdam's urban landscape and separate each neighbourhood from each other, even when surmounted by boulevards. As Frits Palmboom has shown, each former polder remains visible in Rotterdam's urban geography, and each has its own parcelization and orientation. On top of this isolating tendency inherent in the human response to geographic and hydrological realities, certain areas of Rotterdam were developed in conscious isolation: a large portion of the southern docklands were a free trade zone enclosed by a large wall in which duties did not have to be paid, and whole communities were started by shipping companies or shipbuilders (Heijplaat) or later petrochemical industries (Pernis, Hoogvliet) to accommodate their workers.

Moreover, the rich, who strung their boulevards through the expanding city in many other regions and thus created grand allées around which the city could organize itself, often did not live in Rotterdam, as they perceived it as a noxious swamp. They preferred escaping to the dunes west of The Hague. When they did live in Rotterdam, they retreated to small land-tongues sticking out into the former peat bogs of Hillegersberg. Only the Matthenesserlaan remains as a highly fragmented reminder of the grand formality Rotterdam could have had. This social isolation, writ large in the gradual removal of almost all shipping and indus-

Fig I.I   Engraving of Rotterdam by Hesmert 1904
image: Gemeente-archief Rotterdam

try, and thus all workers, to the southern side of the Maas, has left Rotterdam as a city with a strong worker's identity, but not much differentiation or gradation, whether socially, culturally, or economically.

Even the city's core, with its monumental city hall and post office, is an isolated incident. The plans for a grand, beaux-arts-inspired monumental centre, instigated under Mayor Zimmerman in 1913, made it no further than the building of these two structures and a later Stock Exchange along a short boulevard, the Coolsingel, leading to the over-scaled circular Hofplein. The devastation of World War II, including German and Allied bombings, and the subsequent reconstruction of the area in a collage of offices, stores, and pedestrian streets, has left these fragments marooned with no clear relationship to the surrounding areas, to the river, to the station, or to any other recognizable landscape clue, whether natural or human.

This lack of subtlety and connection is also evident in Rotterdam's physical appearance at a smaller scale, as is evident in the mediocre collection of office buildings and housing blocks that make up the city's building stock. This is all the more surprising as this is a city that prides itself in the beautiful design of buildings and objects, from the 1919 City Hall to Oud's worker's housing to Rem Koolhaas's Kunsthal to the absolutely mediocre containers of

capitalism that ring the Weena. And certainly there is great design to be found there. Most notably, the architects who made Rotterdam architecture famous had a sculptural sensibility and an interest in expressing the processes of production that aspired to making their objects more than just isolated boxes. The Van Nelle Factory, with its curved façade drawing one into the factory complex, its ramps connecting the various white-washed blocks, and the intricacy of the connective tissue of hardware that creates coherence through the relationships of the many human bodies using the building, is – or should be – the paradigmatic Rotterdam building. Similarly, the Kunsthal, which unfolds as a continual spiral from the Sea Dike it straddles into a series of galleries barely contained by a collage of structural elements and dividing walls, seems to seek to pull Rotterdam together. Even the NAI building, a late example of that strain of modernism that sought to convolute movement, building and support systems into unstable fragments that would cohere through their intertwining, is exemplary of what Rotterdam architecture could become.

There have also been movements within city planning to see the city as more of a connective tissue. The Hoogstad plan for the River Rotte, only partially carried out, sought to use one of the historic generators of the city as a way of blending housing and communal experience into a singular, always incomplete form. The Piet Blom plan, of which

Aerial-photo of Rotterdam 2001   Fig 1.2
photo:Paul Martens

the Cube Housing is the most visible remnant, did something similar by reconstructing the old harbour, surrounding it with terraced structures, bridging over the four lanes of traffic that lead to downtown, and marking the edge of the market square on the other side of the road. The erection of the various pavilions around the Lijnbaan acknowledged the necessity of occupying the unclaimed space of separation between different planned areas, and the Lijnbaan itself was a heroic attempt to create a connective tissue instead of the introvert shopping enclaves that destroyed so many other cities. In later years, the Prinsenland Plan of 1988 successfully wove existing geography, fauna and parcelization into new housing projects and infrastructure.

But it was not enough. Rotterdam remains a collection of isolated fragments. What one notices more than anything else when one enters the city is the broad River Maas and the large traffic arteries that course through the city. The most heroic structures in the area are not the mid-rise stumps masquerading as skyscrapers, but the giant cranes of a harbour whose centre of gravity is now a good thirty kilometres away from downtown. Only the Erasmus Bridge, itself a connective device, stands as a potent symbol for a new Rotterdam in the city's core. It is itself the largest and most effective example of a collection of superb pieces of architecture that have accumulated in this city of islands since the beginning of the 20th century, helping to establish the reputation both of their architects and of Rotterdam as a place of progressive architecture but nevertheless remaining isolated in this amorphous urban conglomeration.

What then is to be done to create a coherent city out of this collection of beautiful fragments? The answer is relatively simple: the space in-between needs to be designed. This is true all the way from the overall shape of the city to the cobblestones and lighting of the streets. Remarkably enough, there

has not been a clear vision for the city's growth and transformation as a complete entity since the so-called Witteveen plan of the Second World War. The city has grown through accretion, and some of these areas have been beautifully designed, but there has not been a clear sense of what Rotterdam could and should become. A blueprint for the entire region, which was called the 'Rijnmond' or 'Mouth of the Rhine' at one point, would be a good starting point.

It may be that such a plan would discover that Rotterdam itself is a historic artefact that has outlived its usefulness, and that the area should be seen as a collage of neighbourhoods that are part of the much larger 'delta metropolis'. In that case, the connective tissue should be thought of as the transportation systems on a regional and supra-regional scale. The isolated islands of the former Rotterdam would be just part of a puzzle that perhaps demands such isolation as the price for an overall coherence: enclaves for living, working and storage jointly make up a large, vital region.

Let us assume, however, that historical continuity will triumph and Rotterdam will continue to exist. In that case, it will need a plan for its future development that will make it into a coherent and attractive place. Such a plan would have to ask the basic question of how the existing islands can be allowed to develop their own identity, become more con-

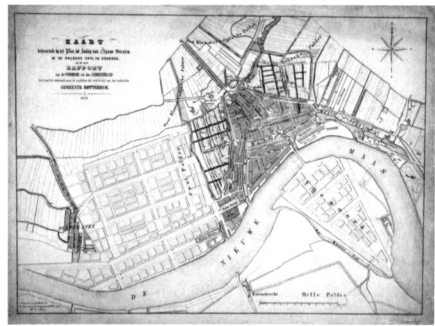

Fig 1.3   Design Rose
image: Gemeente-archief Rotterdam

nected to each other, and be replicated in surrounding areas. At the same time, the city would have to consider that not all of these islands need to be crammed full with housing or offices, and some of the less logical ones, such as former workers' slums that have never worked properly, could and should be given back to nature even as the city continues to expand to meet the demands of a more mobile economy and society. A good example of how the islands might be developed is the Wijnhaven, where thin skyscrapers jostle for position on a thin strip of land. One might contrast this urban fragment with Prinsenland, where the connecting lines to the old city have been strengthened, the old landscape has been preserved and made visible, and new housing creates a clear identity for this suburban location.

As Rotterdam becomes culturally more diverse, the character of each neighbourhood could be developed more. One can imagine urban patterns imported, like the goods in Rotterdam's harbour, from all over the world, and laid out exactly in the islands. A Chinese, a Cape Verdan, a Turkish, and a Polish mini-city could emerge in the various polders that make up Rotterdam.

This is the reverse of the scenario by which the city might dissolve into a larger whole. Again, if Rotterdam is to remain a place as a whole, however, it will need a connective tissue. Obvious places to look for the development of connecting devices

are the great north-south axes. Some of these, such as the area between Schiedam and Vlaardingen and from the lake at Nesselande down to the river, should be strengthened as green corridors. Others, such as the Rivers Rotte and Schie, should be made more accessible and serve as focal points for collective enjoyment of the landscape. Yet others, such as the 'tunnel route' that connects north to south, could be urban boulevards. These are 'easy fixes' that have been proposed previously. The more obvious problem involves how a city that is strung out along the Maas River on an east-west axis can be connected in that direction. There, more radical change may be necessary. The construction of the underground subway during the 1970s was a missed opportunity, as large amounts of buildings were cleared and new boulevards were created above them, but their design was fragmentary and unfriendly to human occupation. The nodes that were meant to connect them, such as the Oostplein, are urban design disasters without scale, direction, or clarity.

Thus this line should be reconsidered as a whole. Another line to the north, running from the Matthenesserlaan, through downtown, up into the newly rebuilt Crooswijk area and out into the expanding suburbs to the east, could help tie the city together at its centre. A third line, running parallel to the railroad lines and highways to the city's north, could then establish a northern axis. While

Fig 1.4 Mathenesserlaan Rotterdam
photo: Anneke Abhelakh

Boompjes Fig 1.5
photo: Anneke Abhelakh

the most southern route could be monumental, and the central one somewhat fragmented and focused on the various ethnic neighbourhoods, the northern one could focus on leisure and infrastructure. The places where the redesigned north-south axes and east-west axes meet should be the place for major public spaces that would have to develop a specific character for Rotterdam as a whole – one that would have to be modern and heroic, recalling the achievements of the business city and the port, but, at the same time, one scaled for human use.

At a smaller scale, Rotterdam needs to redesign its streets and public spaces. At the moment, they are mainly asphalt and concrete. While this metropolis could never become a sylvan city, it could simply use a great deal more green. As cities such as Chicago are showing, this makes sense from an environmental as well as an aesthetic standpoint. One question concerns what the specific landscape architecture of a place such as Rotterdam might be. Can one imagine a vegetation and planting system that would recall the swamps and the polders within the city? The park that Capelle-aan-de-IJssel constructed on its border with Rotterdam might serve as a useful model here, as might Kathryn Gustafson's Westergasfabriekpark in Amsterdam.

But greenery alone will not do the trick. The city needs to develop small-scale structures that will encourage the public to use its spaces. Unlike the previous generation of isolated pavilions, these should be structures that should be attached to existing buildings, bringing the housing and office blocks out of their isolation and down in scale. At places, the city needs to be densified: the Market Square and Museum Park could use housing to define its edges, the Weena and Blaak could use small-scale stores breaking onto the sidewalks.

The architecture of all of this new connective tissue should be both recognizable and open. Rotterdam has established a kind of architecture, most clearly in the modernist collages of the post-war period, which can be built upon. It is an architecture of grids, but also of fragments. It has none of the sculptural heroics of Amsterdam South, but is also clearer in its materiality than most modernist cities. It is, in a strange way, uncomfortable. There is a Rotterdam style, from the strange composition and unfinished symmetries of Maaskant's 1949 Groothandelsgebouw, to the blocks along the Goudse Singel of a few years later, to the buildings of Koolhaas, Mecanoo and Neutelings/Riedijk that wrap up their surroundings into three-dimensional, always unfinished collages. It can and should be continued. The city should resist the construction of isolated, post-modernist towers that have no relationship with this place, but should also not be satisfied with abstract modern monuments. The collage of the new Montevideo Tower and of the Cyclops of the Maritime College are good examples of what is possible – their vertical compositions should be laid out in a horizontal direction, weaving through the city, as the compositions of the post-war reconstruction was.

Pulling this tissue together should be a graphic identity that establishes Rotterdam as a clear presence. This city has nothing like the three crosses that are so unmistakably the mark of Amsterdam.

Fig 1.6   Market square at Blaak Rotterdam
photo: Anneke Abhelakh

Rotterdam's logo is weak, confusing and inconsistent. A few years ago, the graphic design firm 75B proposed a new logo for the city. Something like this could and should be adopted. A graphic identity that captures the city's spirit and is open to its changing demographic and economic make-up could do a great deal to establish a clear communal identity. An expansion of the International Sculpture Collection, with its routes of figural monuments, could also help to establish this sense of shared place.

Finally, Rotterdam is developing as a place of ephemeral events. As a 'festival city' and home to some of the area's largest nightclubs, it has the potential for being a place that blossoms periodically, if not every night. These events should be encouraged, but also brought into relationship to each other. Rotterdam needs more places for collective enjoyment, more informal theatres and places where music can be enjoyed in a less stuffy setting. It also needs bigger festivals, such as the ones organized around the Cultural Capital celebrations of 2001. Perhaps it even needs the Olympics to focus its attention.

All of this may not be enough. Maybe Rotterdam will continue to be a series of islands that will eventually dissolve into the larger collection of multi-nodal urbanization currently known as the Randstad. Perhaps the city will also continue to run away from itself, falling apart into a port out in the North Sea and residential communities closer to The Hague and Gouda than the city core. Perhaps it will become a series of literal islands, as the architect Ronald Wall proposed in his 2001 vision of Rotterdam as an urban delta. But if it still wants to believe it is a city with its own identity and reason to exist as such, it should replicate the experimental spirit and high quality of its isolated buildings in a new urban identity that all its inhabitants and visitors can share.

Fig 1.7   Rotterdam 2001
image: 75B

Progress

FRANK VAN DER SALM

Essay 02

ARCHITECTURE BULLETIN N° 02│2006
The photo essay starts on page:
9-10, 19-22, 39-42, 51-52, 61-64.

Frank van der Salm (1964) is an artist and photographer. The emphasis of his photography shows a gradual shift towards fragments of cities and interiors. The images are recognizable as pictures of a city, but actually which city is never clear. He filters the local identity out of his images, so to speak, and thus makes them abstract. In doing so, he amplifies the obsession with form inherent to architecture. He consciously seeks out the area of tension between portrayal and reality, thereby consistently putting the viewer on the wrong track.

In this photo essay, too, Van der Salm pursues ambivalence. On the one hand his subject matter is what it is: a chronological sequence of images, each autonomous and with an individual, personal impact. On the other hand, Van der Salm grants us a glimpse of his highly personal outlook on architecture, on how a city comes into being, and even on the origin of the metropolis.

In the early 1990s, Van der Salm often photographed landscape, inspired by such examples as Lewis Baltz and Robert Adams in the USA, who, together with Bernd and Hilla Becher in Europe, were the leading exponents of the New Topography. His output has gradually grown more idiosyncratic, and he has shifted his working territory to the city in all its diversity. The hallmark of his style is a deceptive representation of reality, which in effect suggests an alternative reality. He has developed into a photographer who depicts new urban space – as do Olivo Barbieri and Stéphane Couturier, for example, whose work is displayed along with that of Van der Salm in the exhibition *The Spectacular City. Photographing the Future* (NAI, 23 September 2006 to 7 January 2007). Van der Salm's metropolis is recognizable but estranged, abstract yet naturalistic, detailed but synoptic, geographically free and often undetermined. Speaking of his work, he says 'People seldom occur in my images. You, the spectator, are the only person present in the work and hence the sole determiner of photographic reality or unreality.'

– With grateful acknowledgement to MK Galerie, Rotterdam

MODERNISM, AMERICANISM AND HISTORIOGRAPHY

COR WAGENAAR

Cor Wagenaar (1960) is a researcher and writer on architecture, urban planning, history and government policy. He studied history at the University of Groningen and took his doctorate with a thesis about the postwar reconstruction of Rotterdam. In 2001, he was one of the curators of the exhibition *J.J.P. Oud - Philip Johnson, a Dialog* in the NAI, which presented the entire oeuvre of the architect J.J.P. Oud. In 2005, he was involved in the publication of the book *Ideals in Concrete. Exploring Central and Eastern Europe*, which was published in conjunction with the exhibition *Collage Europe* (NAI, 2005).

Spatial Turn

Writing history is a peculiar occupation. The stories historians produce claim to be connected to reality and yet they always remain *Wortgebilde*, constructions of words, which almost always use the passage of time to thread the elements of the story together. *Im Raume lesen wir die Zeit. Über Zivilisationsgeschichte und Geopolitik,*[1] Karl Schlögel claims that this method is rapidly losing its monopoly: besides time, space is once again becoming acceptable as an instrument for comprehending the world around us. Although this *spatial turn* does not augur the end of the narrative – historians will always write stories – it does open up the possibility of examining details which would otherwise probably escape our attention. This is not a new idea: in *Microcosmi*, Claudio Magris describes how history has gradually invaded the

territory of geography 'in the deciphering of signs and furrows in the earth'.[2] He too deals with time in terms of space. Things that are disposed in space are not ordered sequentially, as is usual in historical writing, but simultaneously; and things that are not physically manifest but which determine what is visible also form part of the spatial whole. Schlögel's claim tallies with the recent practices of architectural and urban planning historians, for whom the past is not merely the past but is also part of the present. To these historians, the city of today consists not only of its buildings, roads, parks, pipelines and traffic flows, but also of everything that explains why they came into being. Unlike the conventional historical, textual approach, the *spatial turn* opens up a perspective on alternative histories, which although unexpressed are nevertheless present. This thought is already present in James Joyce's *Ulysses*, although it has never been better articulated than by Robert Musil in his famous novel *The Man Without Qualities* in which he coined the term 'sense of possibility' ('möglichkeitssinn'): 'whoever has it does not say, for instance, "here, this or that has happened, will happen, must happen" but invents "here, this or that might, could, or ought to happen". If he is told that something is the way it is, he will think, "well, it could probably just as well be otherwise". So the sense of possibility could be defined outright as the ability to conceive of everything that might equally well be, and to attach no more importance to what is than to what is not.'

The Hungarian authors György Konrád and Péter Nadás draw a link with the city, which, to them, is a frame narrative in which the stories of the past also speak. It cannot be a coincidence that Magris, Musil, Konrád and Nádas all grew up in Central Europe and that Joyce spent a large part of his life in Trieste, which was the capital of Slovenia until the Italians turned it into one of their outposts. All of them were affected by the dual Austro-Hungarian monarchy, which Musil nicknamed Kakania. Kakania was perhaps the most successful multicultural, multi-ethnic and multi-religious realm ever. It no longer existed, but to Musil's characters its spirit lived on. In Kakania people stood no chance of forgetting that history was spatially determined. In reality, the rock-hard geopolitical frontiers of the former Austro-Hungarian Empire continued to dictate the fate of the inhabitants of this region for a long period. It also applies to the most diverse range of political, economical and cultural trends and movements. However international they tried to be at times, they were never quite able to loosen the grip of the geopolitical frame within which their life played out. Ultimately, space determines not only what happens, but also how its history is written.

If that is true, and if it does not apply only to Kakania, then it must also have had an influence on the development of modernism and in particular on its historiography. That is the theme of this essay, which indeed is no more than an 'essay', an attempt. In the following pages I shall attempt to sketch the outlines of a possible new approach in which the world is no longer read as a text, but rather interpreted more as a multi-layered spatial construction. This essay avoids Kakanian cacophonies of endless digressions and hundreds of notes, and simply presents a possible view. Modernism does not suffer from a lack of dynamism; however, what interests us here is how it is shaped by the way world history draws new borders across the globe. Schlögel's volume can be interpreted in many different ways, but in this essay, geopolitical borders affect the space from the top down. Whether a street is decorated with hammers and sickles, or Coca Cola advertisements, or whether there are social-realist sugar cakes or standardized, mass-produced blocks of flats, is not determined by the inhabitants, the municipality, or national culture, but by the place where superior powers and uncontrollable events defined the borders between the Eastern Bloc and the West.

How did this influence Dutch modernism? We shall limit our survey to the years between 1945 and 1955. At the risk of cutting corners in my argumentation so soon and to prevent this article from taking on Kakanian, that is, unbridled proportions, let us resort to an assumption: if the Iron Curtain did influence Dutch modernism, then the effect may be summed up as Americanization. How

Fig 3.1   Marlene Dietrich on the cover of
LIFE magazine 1948

American is Dutch modernism? The Netherlands sees itself as an outpost of modernism and not only that: it sees itself as belonging to the group of countries responsible for some of modernism's roots. But anyone relying on traditional, historicizing accounts of this subject will not realize that modernism was as good as absent from the Netherlands for a period of at least ten years. The fact that the International Style of the post-war years is at odds with the ideas of the pioneers in many respects would similarly remain underexposed. The reason why modernism staged a comeback at the end of the 1940s, albeit with a fundamentally different character, can apparently be related to the origins of a new, modern reality. This reality indeed turns out to have been geopolitically defined. Modernism in the late 1940s was associated with the new, American, bourgeois lifestyle, and this lifestyle served as a powerful weapon in the Cold War.

Lifestyle as Armament

To gain insight into the post-war reality that prevailed in the Netherlands, it is useful to flick through the pages of the American magazine *Life*. The international edition of *Life* was sold in the Netherlands for 80 Dutch cents, not at all cheap at the time. *Life* presented a view of a lifestyle with all the ingredients that make America American. Through its pages, we bear witness to countless new trends and inventions – the things we now think of as typically American were no less new on the other side of the Atlantic. The fashions, such as T-shirts and bikinis, looked sexy and uninhibited (I doubt if anything similar appeared in the stolid Dutch press of the day). Sneakers, apparently, were a by-product of the tyre industry. Anything to do with cars attracted eager interest. Things that are commonplace today were novel then – self-service gasoline pumps, for instance, were invented in California. In the beginning these new 'gas-a-terias' had hostesses to

demonstrate how to use them. TV came of age and was no longer secondary to the theatre; the roles switched. Jazz was the new music and penetrated everywhere thanks to radio and 78-rpm gramophone records. The image projected here is admittedly something of a cliché, but clichés exist for a reason and they can be extremely potent, as they were in this case. Everything oozed progress: science advanced by leaps and bounds, technology increased human control over nature, and one invention after another made everyday life more comfortable. *Life* invited its readers to take part in a collective adventure, and that is perhaps what made the magazine so appealing.

Woven through this alluring view, though in some respects barely reconcilable with it, are articles projecting a picture of the American business world. This world underwent a managerial revolution in which the interests of the employees became interlocked with those of the company. The aim of the new management style was control. Control, too, seems to have been the underlying theme of the psychological revolution of

Fig. 3.2

those years: the purpose was to get a grip on the unconscious. Corporate man became the stereotype citizen. The lifestyle that glittered in the pages of *Life* was eminently bourgeois, and formed an implicit argument against the socialism that linked progress to the historical role of the working classes. This motif was also characteristic of official propaganda such as the International Circulating Exhibitions curated by New York Museum of Modern Art and is clearly illustrated by the highly successful photographic exhibition *The Family of Man*. Both the managerial revolution and the emphasis on the unity of mankind were consistent with a new culture determined to contrast itself with competing systems.

Contrast is perhaps an understatement: the Communist threat was a major obsession from the early post-war years onwards. The atom bomb and the threat of a Third World War were the flipside of the carefree, elated culture disseminated by *Life*. It was the combination of this image and ultra-conservative militarist rhetoric that made the magazine what it was in those years: the propaganda medium of a lifestyle-at-war. A totally different way of life prevailed on the other side of the Iron Curtain, a lifestyle in which the collective interest was paramount and everyone had to toe the line. There was no jazz or improvisation there, but choral singing and 'the Internationale; no in-dividual spontaneity but the collective march of man towards a better society dictated by historical materialism. This tightly choreographed life was an exact echo of the rhetorical catch-phrases that had been widespread across Europe before the Second World War, and not only under totalitarian regimes. The new American lifestyle seemed like a breath of fresh air in comparison.

The new lifestyle naturally generated a new architecture, one which was forthrightly modern – so modern, in fact, that it sometimes aroused a riot of opposition. Many people could hardly imagine that living in a modern house might be bearable, but those that took the plunge found it was not only possible but could even be pleasant. The *San Francisco Bay* style filled many a magazine page and luxurious villas were everywhere, usually with swimming pools adorned with women in daring bathing costumes. Much attention was focused on the architects Alden Dow and Bruce Goff. *Life* assiduously propagated the modernism of the International Style. And that is hardly surprising: the breakthrough of the International Style was propelled not only by its pragmatic advantages but by the ideological motives implicit in the new lifestyle. In Europe, return to a building style associated with the pre-war society was not opportune – after all, that society could be held responsible for the war and all the misery it had

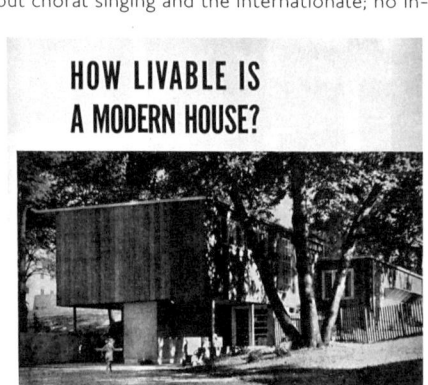

HOW LIVABLE IS A MODERN HOUSE?

Fig 3.3

A Bachelor's House

IT HAS A DANCE FLOOR AND A 50-FOOT POOL

Fig 3.4

entailed. And seeking connections with populist socialist realism, was impossible: it was the style of the enemy. No other option apart from the revised modernism of the International Style presented itself.

The International Style in the Netherlands

The International Style was the bespoke suit for a new culture; it was new not only to Western Europe, but also to the USA itself. This trend shared only a name with the work that was displayed in the famous 1932 exhibition at the New York Museum of Modern Art: the content was utterly different. The International Style manifested itself primarily at points where the Cold War was hottest: in Europe and especially Germany (where Gropius, still clad in army uniform, went in search of his old Bauhaus colleagues to place them in key positions to work on the post-war reconstruction of Germany). We can also use Dutch examples to reconstruct what the International Style entailed and how it related to pre-war modernism. For simplicity, I use the term in this essay to refer to planning as well as architecture. Take suburbanization, for example. Until well into the 1930s, the view in planning circles was that it was difficult, if not impossible, to house workers in satellite towns, far from their place of work. From the fifties onward, urban planning in the Netherlands became increasingly dominated by suburbanization. The more working people became car owners (in the thirties a car would have been an unthinkable luxury), the more rapidly suburbanization progressed. The suburb was seen as the paramount symbol of the American lifestyle, resulting in the rapid Americanization of dwelling in the Netherlands.

Another example is the managerial revolution. This originally typically American phenomenon also made its mark on Dutch urban planning. In the famous *Basisplan voor de Wederopbouw van Rotterdam* (Blueprint for the Post-war Reconstruction of Rotterdam), for example, anything in the earlier post-war reconstruction plan that could not be defended on rational and functional grounds appears to have been eliminated. Urban planning became a form of management, and primarily focused on a rigid, functional zoning in conjunction with a logical road-traffic system. The city manifested itself as the product of a rationalized ground plan with an architectural superstructure; and it is surprisingly clear that in the latter, modernism was not the dominant style until the end of the forties.

In both the suburbanization and the managerialization of urban planning, there are obvious similarities to the USA, without going as far as the direct transplantation of examples from across the Atlantic. After the liberation in 1945, an intensive exchange of knowledge developed between the Netherlands and the USA, leading to numerous study trips. The exchanges, whether relating to industrialization, agriculture or the hotel industry, were always dominated by modern management methods. The spatial planning and architecture that these methods fostered were thus automatically favoured. Consequently architecture and urban planning were emphatically positioned within the framework of national economic planning and rationalization, as pillars for the construction of a new society. There is no doubt that the world view propagated by *Life* magazine was the perfect expression of that society.

Finally, we have the architecture of the International Style. I already noted that its inherent innovations had little in common with the pre-war European modernism that had been the focal point of the famous American exhibition of 1932. They were all the more bound up with the American adventure. The image of the lifestyle was cheerful, carefree, light, bright, free and natural – and as far as habitation is concerned, suburban. Against the background of ruins and empty bomb-sites that disfigured cities all over Europe until well into the 1950s, the architecture of the new shops, garages, petrol stations, theatres, cinemas, and villas struck a joyful note. Decoration and representation, two phenomena which the pioneers of pre-war modernism sometimes passionately tried to eliminate, were evidently accepted without trouble. Many buildings were decorated by sculptures whose form seems related to the abstract art popular at the time. The International Style is the style of the consumer society as collective ideal – something completely different from the individualistic consumerism of today – and it is striking that the joy of liberation is most prominent in building projects that represented this new ideal. Apart from this, modernization processes also occurred in the public housing sector, but these were primarily in relation to industrialization, typology, and standardization. The break with pre-war modernism was far less obvious in this sector; or was it that this kind of modernized production process had been rare and experimental before the war but now suddenly dictated the style of housing everywhere? This would explain the difference between American and Dutch suburbs in terms of appearance: the former consist mainly of one-family houses, the latter of rows of low-rise interspersed with walk-up and high-rise apartment blocks.

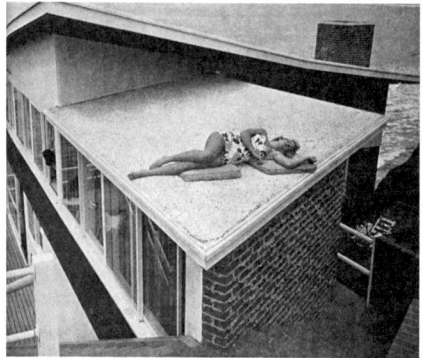

BACHELOR'S RETREAT JUTS OVER SURF

Fig 3.5   "Bachelor's retreat juts over surf"

Modern myths

Once the Iron Curtain forced the Netherlands politically closer to the USA, Dutch architecture and urban planning began to Americanize. That the Dutch espoused the International Style is beyond argument. The distance between this new style and pre-war modernism is hardly any less than that between all the other pre-war movements. This makes it impossible to explain the almost universal acceptance of the International Style as an internal development within modernism. It may seem paradoxical, but acceptance of the style clearly benefited from its image of normality and continuity, two sides of the same coin. Traditional historiography also played a large part by implying that the architecture and urban design of the post-war reconstruction era was a rational response to the need to clear up the devastation and build a new society. But this angle denies the historical implications of the International Style's breakthrough (logically, if it were the only option available there would be no point in discussing it). Another drawback is that it represents the period between the pioneering work of the twenties and early thirties, which never made up more than a few percent of the total architectural output, and the universal modernism of the 1950s, as an insignificant interlude. Moreover, the emphasis on a direct line that is supposed to run through such movements as De Stijl, De 8 en Opbouw to that of the International Style suggests that the roots of the latter lay in the Netherlands and that it was not a product of multiple external influences. The Dutch State also tried to play this card, by cooperating on an exhibition dedicated to De Stijl at the Museum of Modern Art in New York, for example – to the fury of some of the old members of this movement, who opposed attempts to represent De Stijl as a purely Dutch movement. The United States of America was seldom referred to in the propaganda for the new architecture and planning, probably no more than before the war.

Instead, the social character, the scientific foundations, rationality, and the contribution to the construction of a new community were emphasized. However, it is easy to recognize the American influence in the look of the new lifestyle. It is also obvious that this lifestyle formed a stark contrast with the Communist society on the other side of the Iron Curtain where, it was often suggested, the lack of freedom, censorship and totalitarian control was not all that different from the repression people here knew first-hand: National Socialism. This gave the new architecture and planning a moral and ideological charge, a special feature of which was that it did not use any of the familiar political-rhetorical propaganda devices, but promoted an attractive new lifestyle instead – namely the lifestyle embodied by the International Style. Finally, what is striking, if understandable, is that most of the pioneers of pre-war modernism were glad to accept the International Style being interpreted as their legacy, thereby retrospectively confirming themselves in their avant-garde role. Only a few of them disavowed any link between the pre-war and post-war work, while most modernist designers exerted themselves to stress the connection. In doing so, they were able to place their stamp on the first generation of published historical surveys of architecture that dealt with the origins and developments of the modern movement. These books rarely referred to the decline of this movement and, when they did so, they explained it away as having been caused by the rise of the populist totalitarianism of the Soviet Union and Nazi Germany, thereby underlining modernism's moral superiority. This superiority converged with that of the new lifestyle and, although the American inspiration was implicitly recognized, it was not highlighted too much.

New history?

There can thus be no doubt that the historiography is in need of revision. Mindful of the 'lessons' of Schlögel, while of course starting from an entirely individual interpretation of them, the new historiography should acknowledge that the new concept of spatial containers has greater explanatory power than merely attempting to chart stylistic genealogies. Stylistic choices are partly determined by space. Insofar as geopolitical spaces converge with ideological systems – as was certainly the case during the Cold War – these also delimit propagandistic and historiographical spaces within which missionary work has a higher priority than presenting an adequate historical picture. Such a picture will have to be built anew from the ground up.

THE OUTDOORS IS USED, RESPECTED

MODERN ARCHITECTURE is popular. This is the first low-cost house designed by the famed Frank Lloyd Wright, who was born in Richland Center, Wis.

Fig 3.6 "Modern architecture is popular."

BEGINNERS occasionally have a little trouble with the gas hose despite simplified nozzle, and need help. The girls mop up spilled gas immediately to diminish fire hazard.

Fig 3.7 "Beginners occasionaly have a little trouble with the gas hose…"

NATION'S BIGGEST HOUSEBUILDER

Fig 3.8

– All the visual material in this essay comes from *Life* magazine 1947–48.

What does the *spatial turn* mean for the city – for its streets, its buildings, its squares? These features lose the self-evident interpretation they formerly drew from stories of the rise and fall of movements and tendencies. The *spatial turn* leads to a historicization of space, which becomes a playing field of varying interests, interpretations, ambitions, philosophies, theories, insights, responsibilities and, above all, choices, in which the reality that is created crystallizes out from the world of other possibilities as a whole, which hence also comes into play. What seem to be disconnected stylistic fragments built during the first phase of post-war reconstruction in Rotterdam, for instance, are now interpretable: references to Italy or (especially) Perret turn out to have been mainstream for a while, a kind of mid-century Modern, which only gave way to the International Style during the Cold War. So it becomes possible to reassess this style as a manifesto for a joyful, liberated new world.

NOTES

1 Karl Schlögel, ‚Im Raume lesen wir die Zeit. Über Zivilisationsgeschichte und Geopolitik' ('In Space We Read Time. On the History of Civilization and Geopolitics'), Munich 2003,

2 Claudio Magris, 'Microcosmi' , Amsterdam 1998 (original publication 1997), p. 205[??].

RESOURCES

– Luce, H.R. (ed.), Life, Chicago, Time, 1936-2000.
– Magris, C., Microcosmi, Amsterdam, Bakker, 1998 (1997).
– Musil, R., Der Mann ohne Eigenschaften, Reinbek bei Hamburg, Rowohlt, 1987 (1930).
– Schlögel, K., Im Raume lesen wir die Zeit: über Zivilisationsgeschichte und Geopolitik, München, Hanser, 2003.

Landscape as a Living Artwork

Proposals for a National Museum

DIRK SIJMONS

Essay 04

ARCHITECTURE BULLETIN N° 02│2006

We are getting a National Historical Museum. That is what we heard recently at the presentation of the annual budget. I've been asked to think about this subject before. Then, it was at the invitation of the literary journal *De Gids* in response to a call from the national daily the *NRC Handelsblad*, on the cusp of the magical year 2000, to select 'the artwork of the millennium'. As was to be expected, the number of Bach and Rembrandt nominations was high. However, it was also striking that a number of entries proposed the Dutch landscape because 'we have worked on it together for the whole millennium'. This work of art cannot be omitted from a National Museum.

Why has the honour of acting as a virtual guest curator been conferred on a landscape architect rather than a historian? Is it perhaps because the Dutch landscape has been divided into different historical disciplines? Historical geographers have the genesis of the agrarian cultural landscape (landscape history) as the object of their research; the art historians focus on the designed landscape, rural areas, country estates, land reclamation and polders; the archaeologists look primarily at the earliest periods of human occupation; finally, the palaeo-ecologists concentrate on the period before the (dominant) influence of mankind. A profound rivalry exists

Dirk Sijmons (1949) graduated from the Architecture Faculty of Delft University of Technology and, in 1989, established H+N+S Landschapsarchitecten together with Lodewijk van Nieuwenhuijze and Dick Hamhuis. This partnership won the Prince Bernard Cultuurfonds Prize for Applied Art and Architecture in 2001 for its work in the field of water planning, nature development design, and regional design. Dirk Sijmons was awarded the prestigious Rotterdam-Maaskant Prize for his contributions to theory, publications, social debate and public information on landscape architecture and urban planning. Since 2004, he has been the Netherlands State Advisor on Landscape.

between the first two disciplines in particular: the historical geographers and the art historians. The divisive question is whether the history of the Dutch landscape is predominantly a traditional agrarian history of cultivation, or whether the history of ideas is the dominant factor. By choosing a landscape architect as curator, this rivalry is stripped of its disciplinary acuteness and the emphasis is shifted to a more pragmatic approach, which recognizes and considers scientific perspectives and then tries to incorporate them. Of course, the question that must be addressed by the National Museum programme is that concerning the extent to which the Dutch landscape has been formed from the bottom up or from the top down.

The National Museum needs to get the Dutch to take a fresh look at what has become so obvious they rarely notice it any more. But, like any national museum, it also needs to attract foreign visitors, if only to be able to operate financially. This is a good thing, because 'landscape' (from *landschap*) is one of the few words from Dutch that has penetrated other languages. Once outside built-up areas, many Dutch imagine themselves to be 'in nature'. This misunderstanding cannot be simply dismissed with a lament about modern city-dwellers who have become alienated from the surrounding agricultural land. This view is all the more extraordinary because this is a country in which the landscape is utterly artificial, right down to the smallest detail. Foreigners spot this straight away: the Portuguese tourist who, in the *Vrij Nederland* magazine, described the highpoint of his stay in the Netherlands as 'a journey through a Mondrian painting', suffered no illusions about the distinction between landscape and nature. Is this confusion the expression of a desire for 'nature' on the part of a largely urban population? Have we become so used to mentioning landscape and nature in the same breath over the last hundred years that the words have become interchangeable? Or perhaps the imagined relationship between people and nature, as surveyors and landscape architects have fashioned it in country estates down through the centuries, has lost so much of its expressive power that 'real nature' has been reduced to these landscapes? Whatever the case, an essential element in society seems to have been lost in the relationship between citizen and landscape. If we want a decent public discussion about landscape, we must first relearn how to 'read' it as a cultural expression. More reading will turn out to be extraordinarily rewarding: society will once again be able to take pleasure from the constructability of topography.

The reader has been warned: in the hands of this guest curator, the programme for the landscape department of the National Museum will take on an unadulterated cultural-political character. And both the National Museum and landscape will be instrumentalized to this end.

As it lies, the Dutch landscape is, of course, a living artwork. It is one big Holland Festival in which the various layers of history are often still legible, especially to connoisseurs. However, the processes are going so slowly that we will soon be able to use the institution of the Museum to make the conceivable in the long-term. As soon as we want to honour the artwork by visiting it, walking it, we find ourselves up against a major problem. Whereas our nature reserves have been gradually opened up to visitors, it is rare for this to happen with the landscape. Landscape does not function as public, collective space. Large areas are still locked away. We estimate that land consolidation (*ruilverkaveling*) and the proj-

Fig 4.1   Musée de l'Histoire Naturelle in Paris
photo: Daniël Gonzalez

ects over the last 50 years aimed at redesigning the landscape have led to at least 30,000 kilometres of unmetalled roads, drove roads, church paths and similar tracks being lost. These paths are not privatized, but have arisen culturally and, consequently, simply disappear. It should be a top government priority, within the framework for the National Museum, to reinstate the fine mesh of paths across the landscape. This would make the landscape more accessible and — a beneficial side-effect — provide the infrastructure for the much-desired broadening of the rural economy by bringing together the producers (farmers) and the consumers (city dwellers). And it would be a blessing if this new infrastructure were to be left free of all the coloured posts, notice boards and signs found on all other rural bridle, cycle and footpaths in the Netherlands. Then we would be able to wander and lose our way. For those of you with reservations who are asking yourselves how this could possibly work in the Netherlands with its apparently indispensable supply of information, we now have the first useful application of the Global Positioning System (GPS). This can precisely locate walkers, who will be able to use their mobile phones to link into a database in the National Museum to request information about the landscape history of the place they find themselves in, including local tales. Once the straying and going astray becomes tedious, walkers will be able to request route information. Magnificent bonfires of all the defunct boards and signposts could be built across the regions.

Before we enter the permanent exhibition in the Netherlands National Museum, to orientate ourselves we shall first visit the Musée de l'Histoire Naturelle in Paris. This museum, originally built in the nineteenth century, has recently been renovated and expanded, or rather, transformed, by the architect Alexandre Chemetoff. The museum is an excellent and imposing reference for the atmosphere, scenes, and impact we see before us. Chemetoff has left the existing museum completely intact, with its endless succession of dusty galleries lined with beautiful walnut cabinets in which one drawer after the other reveals dazzling collections of beetles or butterflies; the cases with stuffed and preserved animals in a permanent state of over population; the mysterious anatomical details and the rooms with reconstructed skeletons. Chemetoff has thus preserved from extinction this way of archiving and viewing. The new wing is attached to the old museum. The message this wing communicates dawns only slowly on the museum visitor. The first impression is dazzling.

Every animal, from the exotic tropical land snail to the most insignificant insect, is illuminated in its own magnificent showcase; the suction of air from the glass lift doors opening and closing causes the birds suspended in the lift shafts to move as if soaring along thermals streams; the larger stuffed animals are exhibited two-by-two in a fabulous parade down the central hall. This over-aestheticization initially gives rise to a great sense of wonder until one's sensory perception switches to the crushing sensation that everything we still have on Earth is dead and here in this museum; that we are looking at the preserved remnants of the wealth of species: the museum as Noah's Ark. Having been addressed by this, literally, *architecture parlante*, the visitor can go in two directions in his or her emotions: sorrow and resignation at the loss, or rebelliousness and activism – we must do something before this becomes reality.

Our museum will evoke a comparable ambiguous feeling, not about the animal kingdom, but about the collective and cultural élan. The Dutch landscape is beautiful and unique, but it derives its mysterious appeal primarily from the amazement and admiration with which we regard the results of collective acts by dozens of generations. It is never completely a co-production between human activity and the powers of nature with complicated symbolic references between culture and nature. This amalgamation of a history of hydraulics, diligent land reclamation, and a solid pattern of urbanization has generated the first inhabited and cultivated megastructure. The question that will be indirectly posed is whether we are still in a position to resuscitate this collective ambition, or whether this chapter has been closed for all time? Are we still capable of creating landscapes, or do we have to make do with attempts to fix the landscapes our predecessors left us and to stand by and watch powerlessly as what were once clear, historical, landscape images slowly fade?

The landscape department is housed in a separate pavilion at a decent distance from the main building of our National Museum. It consists of a central hall, the starting point, with corridors configured around it. The central hall is one of the attractions of the museum. A multimedia show demonstrates the genesis of each landscape type. The area around the rivers, the coastal zone, the peat regions, the surface-sand landscapes and the hills of Limburg are all presented within an hour. The show begins with an animation of the prehistory of our territory from 200,000 BC to the earliest habitation. From that moment, visitors are able to zoom in on any type of landscape they choose. Vividly detailed maps of the most typical or spectacular regions

Fig 4.3   Naturalis
image: H+N+S Landschapsarchitecten

illustrate the story of land reclamation, water control, and occupation. In an hour the visitor can see how this landscape came
into being. Reconstructions clearly illustrate how natural history
follows cultural history: types vanish or appear, become rarer or
more common, as a natural expression of human activity in the
different periods.

Another screen demonstrates the most important social influences on landscape formation: from tribes and clans, through
feudalism and the organization of common land, to the drainage
of peat areas by the church, commercial peat extraction, water
boards, provinces, and the rise of the centralized state. The history
of technology is also part of the programme with a lot of focus
on technologies for controlling water (early dike systems, dams,
windmills and sluices, up to contemporary techniques) and agricultural technologies (from crop rotation to the discovery of artificial fertilizer). Dominant patrons from each period are depicted:
the churches and monasteries in the Middle Ages; commercial
peat excavation and urban capital which financed the drainage
and the construction of country estates in the sixteenth and seventeenth centuries; King Willem I and the (National) Water Board
in the nineteenth century; land consolidation and land division in
the twentieth century. Histograms track demographic developments, agricultural productivity, labour deployment per hectare
and the level of urbanization down the ages. Grippingly realistic
films make life in the different periods almost tangible.

The gallery has a second floor with a glass dome. The Dutch sky,
which to a considerable degree defines the image of the Dutch
landscape, displays itself above a panoramic strip on which a
Photoshop compilation of Ruysdael paintings has been composed,
leading out to the horizon. The dome can be closed like a plan-

Fig 4.4 Naturalis Culturalis
image: H+N+S Landschapsarchitecten

etarium so that in the evenings, or in the event of dull skies, different cloud formations can be projected onto it, perhaps accompanied by an explanation from the weatherman.

In the area between the landscape pavilion and the main building are examples of historical gardens. Here visitors may rest and meditate in an enclosed monastery garden, stroll through the formal gardens of the seventeenth century when garden art was still highly regarded as a means of expression, eat a sandwich in an English-style garden, forage through the nature gardens of the twentieth century, or rest on a bench in gardens of the new sobriety. This area presents a welcome opportunity for a breath of fresh air after the exertions of the national history programme.

A long corridor through these style gardens joins the pavilion to the main building. Both walls are hung with borrowed works by landscape painters and photographers. An unusual cut through art history has been made for this display. On the left are painters and photographers who mainly allowed themselves to be led by emotion and intuition. Melancholy and nostalgia play an important part here. On the right are artists who to a large extent take rationality and logic as their points of departure. In this category, idealism and (later) future thinking are often the key words.

Candidates for the left-hand wall are Hobbema and Van der Neer from the seventeenth century and Van Strij and Koekkoek from the eighteenth century; the nineteenth century is represented by perhaps the entire Hague School and the twentieth century by De Ploeg, with its hyperbolic idealization of the Groningen landscape, and by such artists as Benner and Cremer. A photographer typical of the left-hand wall would be Martin Kers. The author Geert Mak will lead a guided tour once a week to tell us what had already left Jorwerd before God did. (*Jorwerd: The Death of the Village in Late Twentieth-Century Europe*, 1996.)

In a similar chronology, the right-hand wall presents Ruysdael (the landscape presenting the city), Cuyp, de Moucheron, Gestel, Knip, Vester, Van Looij and, from modern times, Permeke (sharp criticism of the lot of agricultural workers) and a new view of the early work of Mondriaan. The photographic master that typifies the right-hand wall is Rem Koolhaas, who here issues the punishment for the claim that, in a heterotopical, generic city, only the void is left for us to design. In view of the fact that quite a lot still happens in the Dutch void, he will be allowed to demonstrate this in a weekly tour. The corridor not only provides access to the pavilion, but also folds itself around it, so that the visitor can choose to go left or right. To the left, the history of the preservation landscape unfolds, starting with Romanticism, when the preservation of the Forest of Fontainebleau by Rousseau and his followers found its echo in the Netherlands in Van Eden's attempts to preserve Beekburger Forest. This is followed by the interesting personal unions between the hygienists (who propagated nature and the landscape as medicine for urban maladies), the founders of Natural Monuments, and the early thinkers in urban planning, who heralded the start of preservation. There is the rift in the movement in the 1930s over the attitude towards land reclamation as work for the unemployed (refuse, or take part and lead). The 1950s to 1980s are represented by the rise of the idea that the preservation of nature and the landscape is a task for government. The role of the government within the framework of unrelenting land consolidation proved insufficiently effective in preventing the once strong historical image of the Dutch landscape from slipping through our fingers like sand. Government bills such as the Relation

Bill (*Relatienota*, 1975, on the relationship between farmers and nature) and the Belverdère Bill (1999, also on a relationship, but this time between environmental and spatial planning and cultural history) mark the end of this line.

To the right, the visitor encounters the history of ideas of landscape. The seventeenth-century plans for the drainage of the Beemster, Purmer and Wormer lakes in North Holland clearly illustrate how the surveyors responsible managed to combine beauty and utility before the original sin of labour division. Here, all jostling together, are plans for the large estates, the eighteenth and nineteenth-century English landscape style, early twentieth-century examples of care of the landscape by the Dutch Forestry Commission along trunk roads and canals, the later expansion of the field of action by the landscape architects of the land consolidation (the construction of the landscape as the counterpoint, which broke away in the 1930s, to landscape preservation) and, of course, the consideration of the Zuiderzee polders. A presentation of landscape ideas from the various Spatial Planning bills – the newer the thicker, the thicker the more ineffective – complete the line.

Two semicircular walkways rejoin each other beyond the central hall. Here begins the new corridor, which is dedicated to future visions of the cultural landscape. The left wall addresses the question of how we might treat cultural heritage. The visitor is confronted with a row of six doors, with 'Canonize' written on the first and 'Ignore' on the last. Behind the first door, which promises the fixing of the canonical heritage, a set of stairs leads down to an underground corridor which takes us back to the exhibit about Dutch national history in the National Museum. A small exhibition in this corridor clearly demonstrates that canonizing landscape is virtually impossible. The defining elements of Dutch landscape are, after all, so close to its (agrarian) use that the strict preservation of the landscape in the context of changing uses is so difficult to achieve that it might sooner be compared to conserving historical interiors than to preserving town and village views. If visitors persevere in this choice, they will find themselves stuck in a loop in the museum, which may only be broken by the security guard locking up. Behind the door 'Ignore' is another set of stairs which leads down to a creepy cellar housing projects that convey the existing landscape as a *tabula rasa*, with a curious collection of scale models of investment ruins. On the other four doors, in curly letters, are the words 'Museumize', 'Commericalize', 'Regionalize', and 'Modernize'. On the other side of these doors are four cabinets, each presenting a different cultural attitude to landscape heritage, and each time with a different dose of preservation and development. These are linked by semi-concealed corridors, which cannot be closed. It is obvious that no one, not even the government, which governs over an ever-more pluriform society, can impose any one of these four options. The future consists of all four, in a precisely proportioned mix of their strong points, with the emphasis being different each time, depending on the circumstances and desires.

On the right-hand wall the different scenarios are hung across the large areas of our time. They lift the corner of the veil, for instance, on the consequences for the landscape of changes in agriculture, which hang like a dark cloud over it. They explain such questions as: How should we supervise these transformations and will the cows remain in the fields? There are also scenarios around the significance of the development of nature for the landscape, interpreted as a twenty-first century cultural design assignment. After all, it is always about finding a new way to stage nature and to reinstate it in a controlled way in our highly developed country by strengthening the view of our landscape's cultural aspect. Furthermore, we also find scenarios about the continuous process of urbanization, which is forcing difficult choices to be made regarding the red-green configuration we want in the future metropolis. And then there is the necessity to respond to climate change and rising sea levels. The water programme this is leading to is the only thing, as a new, collective task, that is in a position to generate new landscape structures.

At the end of this corridor we enter a spacious cabinet. The left and right lobes of the brain, which in the rest of the corridor network were separated, are joined here in a synthesis in which an optimal co-operation between emotion and reason, useful suspicion and development-minded thought is desperately desired. The cabinet contains a few studies of future landscapes, in a somewhat dreamlike setting, where loving treatment of the heritage is coupled with 'major programme points' which are designed in such a way that they form a meaningful contribution to the cultural landscape.

In this final cabinet we ask ourselves the existential question about the formation of landscape. Are we still capable of making it? Are we still able to make landscape consciously and without shame? Or does the corridor to the future reach a dead end in the cabinet of the beautiful illusion? Precisely at the moment we ponder this question we notice another door, unadorned, which seems to be intended to blend in with the wall. 'Service Exit' is inscribed on a simple sign. Before we realize what we are doing we have pushed open the door. The next moment we are suddenly standing there, far away from the National Museum, in the middle of the country, in the middle of the living artwork. Again the question: Are we still capable of making it?

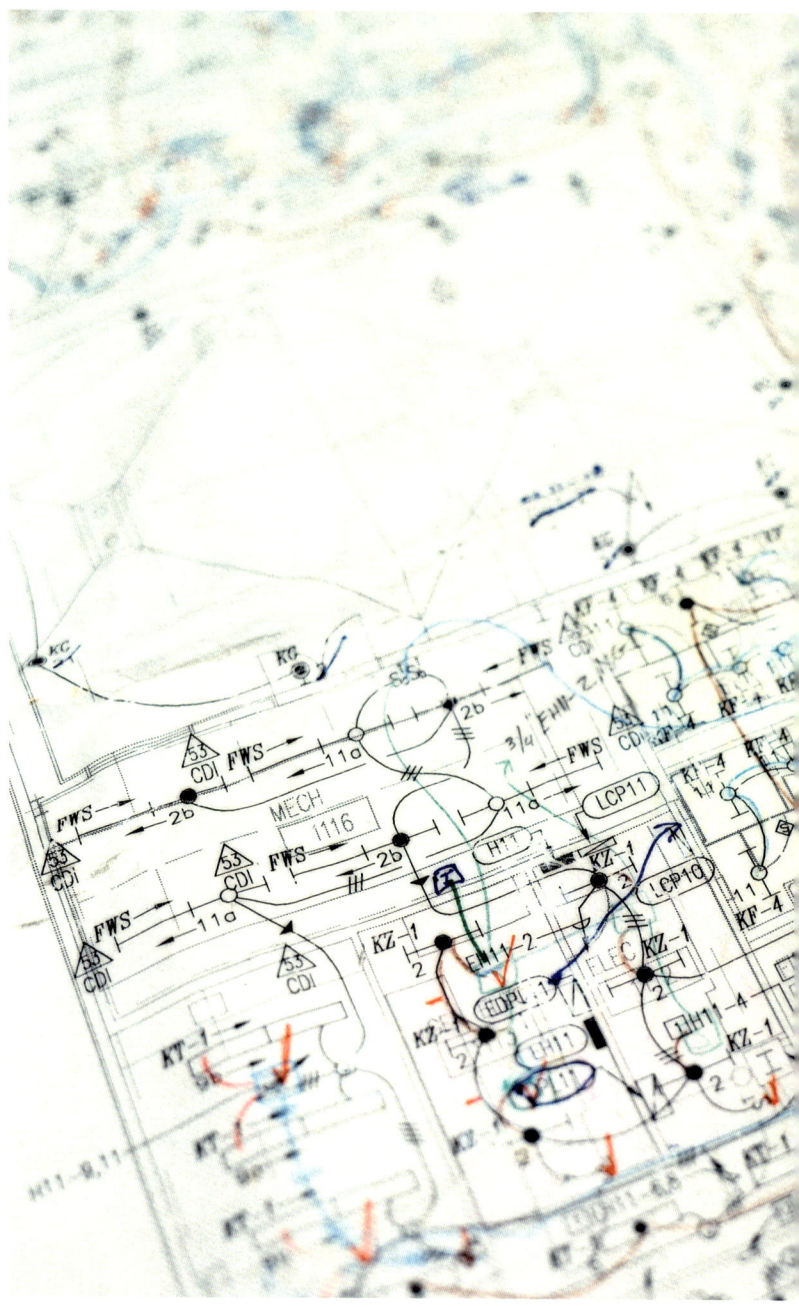

Facts on the Ground

URBANISM FROM THE MIDDLE OF THE ROAD TO THE DITCH

Michelle Provoost & Wouter Vanstiphout

Essay 05

ARCHITECTURE BULLETIN N° 02 | 2006

Of his biggest hit, 'Heart of Gold', Canadian singer Neil Young wrote, '*This song put me in the middle of the road. Travelling there soon became a bore, so I headed for the ditch. A rougher ride but I saw more interesting people there.*'[1]

Worldwide, where hundreds of millions of people live their lives in urban conditions far removed from the professional spotlights, the Ditch School of Urban Design is developing. This disparate school shares one strand of DNA: the emancipatory, collectivist, anti-conformist, break-through élan of the Modern Movement in its 'heroic age'. These practices have shed the stylistic consensus of Modernism but share an attitude about their different urban contexts: they are driven by ideologies and civic goals that seem positively old-school. Most of them, like members of a secret international brotherhood, know each other. The Urban Think Tank in Caracas, Venezuela, artist Jeanne van Heeswijk in the Netherlands, The Center for Urban Pedagogy (CUP) in New York, Rahul Mehrotra and the Urban Design Research Institute in Mumbai, City Min(e)d in Belgium, Public Architecture in San Francisco, Atelier Bow-Wow in Japan, the Everyday Urbanism group in the U.S., and Stalker in Italy are some of the groups that invent and realize their own projects from outside official institu-

Michelle Provoost (1964) and Wouter Vanstiphout (1967) are co-founders of Crimson Architectural Historians in Rotterdam. Their partnership participates in and initiates projects involving research and planning relating to the twentieth century and the contemporary city. Since 1999, Provoost and Vanstiphout have lead WiMBY!, an experimental project for the systematic regeneration of Hoogvliet, a dilapidated satellite municipality of Rotterdam.

tions and client-architect-budget relations, analyzing existing social and spatial situations and retrofitting them with programmes that bring their particular ideal version of reality a little closer. These practices don't wait for a client or a commission – they forge ahead on their own and find other ways to finance the project.

Their projects often rely on maniacal commitment to one city or neighborhood; they dive in and dig up everything possibly useful for their intended projects and hold on until there is at least one 'fact on the ground', one realization of their intentions that proves their ideas viable and prepares the way for more. These offices, groups, and artists have abandoned the idea of the conventional architects' office or urban planning department and have blurred the boundaries between urban planning, urban design, art, and social work. They don't care how they are classified as long as their projects work to some extent. To us, they are urbanists much more than the Italianate-square-designing or pseudo-avantgarde-vision-conceiving architects who have hijacked City Hall and Academia. Having headed for the ditch, they do not allow themselves to become distracted by the insatiable hunger of clients and magazines for glossy images and good-looking design. They engage with some condition neglected by the officials or professionals, and they explore and analyze its real social and cultural lineaments. They use design to visualize issues and solve problems. These offices all believe that the community-forming power of their interventions is often inversely proportional to their physical impact and the size and their financial investment. They make strategic gestures which prove a point, which show a deep political understanding of their urban contexts and are designed to change these dynamics from within. Their interventions can be physical objects but, even then, they are more importantly tactical manipulations of political landscapes. By succeeding in building something, these offices change the political status quo in such a way that more things become thinkable and enactable. Let's examine three examples of Ditch Urbanism.

Urban Think Tank, Caracas

One of the most politically outspoken of this new kind of practice is the Urban Think Tank in Caracas. Led by two architects trained at Columbia University, the Venezuelan Alfredo Brillembourg and the Austrian Hubert Klumpener, UTT has shifted its attention from the formal city of blueprints, commissions, clients, and international attention to the informal city, with its slums, its millions of impoverished 'clients', its isolation from global capital, and its illegal status.[2] UTT states that in 'the glob-

al South' this urban condition is ubiquitous and requires serious study and new design tools. UTT does not condemn the slums as illegal and dangerous, as do Caracas's planning agencies and real estate entrepreneurs. Neither do they pity slum dwellers as trapped in refugee camps for the disenfranchised which need to be replaced by something else, as do NGOs and development-aid agencies. Instead, they describe the slums as another city: just as rich, exciting, and sociologically and economically fertile as the formal one, maybe more so. Klumpener and Brillembourg maintain that the informal city is not illegal, it is extra-legal; having no city hall, post office, or telephone company, it falls outside the standard organizational networks. But it is here to stay; its economy is huge and deeply rooted; it is more sustainable than the formal city, being almost 100% pedestrian and producing less than half the garbage. The informal city makes up 50% of the main urban areas in the global South but has hardly garnered architectural and urbanistic attention. It demands and produces another kind of urban design: first the occupation of land, then building, then planning, then attainment of ownership rights.

UTT has translated the phenomenology of the informal city, which it has mapped and analyzed extensively, with Caracas as *pars pro toto*, into an urban practice that is showing its first results. One of their projects is the *Vertical Gym*

Fig 5.1 UTT Interior Vertical Gym Caracas,
Venezuela 2004
photo: Urban Think Tank

Fig 5.2 UTT Exterior Vertical Gym Caracas,
Venezuela 2004
photo: Urban Think Tank

where there used to be a soccer field in the dense Barrio La Cruz. Extending and exploiting a proven need, UTT used the existing sports field to construct a community building with spaces for the city health department, a road, basketball courts, a dance studio, a weightlifting area, the office of the municipal sports director, a running track, a rock-climbing wall, and a rooftop soccer field. The complex, interwoven structure can be used for cultural and entertainment events at any time. The project was designed and built by UTT workers, some of it with their own hands, using a sophisticated and cheap construction technique. Afterwards it was simply given to the community, which started to plan its use, acquire its ownership, etc. With this and other small projects, UTT is knitting the fragments of Caracas into one megacity, equipped with architectural gadgets like community meeting houses and a rainwater retention basin, and connectors like pedestrian bridges and steps that will enable it to function better. Theirs is an urban vision of maximum ambition that is being implemented slowly but surely in total separation from the official master plans for Caracas. Just like the urban blueprints of the 1950s and 1960s, it is also based on a thorough survey of what makes this city tick; but it has the assumption that its solutions and conclusions can be repeated elsewhere. The difference in scale of design and investment of public power between a project like the Vertical Gym or a modernist urban scheme by, say, Jose Luis Sert, for a South American Metropolis is staggering. On a conceptual level however, the approaches share the scale of the metropolis as a single organism. According to UTT, the seemingly unplannable megacity can be steered and influenced by the smart deployment of spatial tools, spread out strategically over the city and thereby 'knitting' it together. The Gym proves a point about the urban performance of barrios, favelas and slums, of which there are tens of thousands over the globe; this small project can be said, therefore, to even supercede the urban scale of its modernist forefathers and to attain a global scale of urbanity.

Rahul Mehrotra, Mumbai

A similar approach to the informal city is being implemented by Rahul Mehrotra, an architect with a practice in Mumbai who is also a professor of architecture at the University of Michigan, Ann Arbor.[3] Like Klumpener and Brillembourg, Mehrotra sees his city as a unique place with traits that are ubiquitous in the contemporary urban world. Therefore he exhaustively analyzes Mumbai and presents it as a showcase for the failure of official urbanism and as a huge laboratory for the invention of new urbanistic tools. Whereas UTT uses the term *informal city*, Mehrotra uses the term *kinetic city*. In doing so, he turns our gaze from the immense building projects on the Mumbai waterfront to what is happening on the sidewalks and at wedding parties and other festivities. Mehrotra has analyzed the ways a street trader occupies a piece of sidewalk and then, by gradually adding more and larger physical elements, ends up with a little building on the street. The process of occupation, building, and ownership runs exactly parallel to the processes described by UTT in Caracas. Mehrotra does not limit himself to the illegal, or the semi- or extra-legal, or the poor. Another important reality for him is wedding parties, for which lavishly decorated, architecturally camp halls and venues are being built, used, and taken down in two to three days. The city of brick and mortar is a hardly-visible substructure that sustains an effervescent city of cloth, bamboo, neon lights, laser beams, and ecstatic dancing. Mehrotra studies the dense informal networks of people travelling through the city carrying hot lunches from homes to workplaces at the speed of a motorized courier on a traffic-free day.

One of Mehrotra's ongoing projects is in a neo-classical district of colonial Mumbai that normally would be either threatened with demolition and new construction or with museum-like conservation. Both options would create a one-sided vision, fixing the district in one era and identity. As part of his innovative urban conservation strategy, Mehrotra has organized an art festival, building on the large concentration of art galleries in the area, using it to draw visitors and raise the attractiveness of the area. In this way not only awareness of the cultural and historical significance of the district was reached, but money was also raised to preserve the buildings. Many small interventions in public space were made, thereby choreographing the kinetic urban elements to revive this area and dramatize its strange conflict between classical urban spaces and the fast, exciting rhythms of contemporary Mumbai. Mehrotra's reversed strategy to first revitalize public space and raise money to conserve the historic buildings in the process has proven more succesful than the conventional conservationist's method. His interest as an architect/conservator/urbanist does not lie with physical spaces or architectural history, but rather with the palimpsest of meanings and functions, the contradictory identities of this city. He does not seek or find his commissions or clients in the government or in large real estate investment agencies, but rather in the 'deep democracy' of local NGOs, slum-dweller unions, and informal organizations. Whereas 'normal' or 'middle of the road' architects and planners tap into the power source of public authority

Fig 5.3 'Kala Ghoda', regenerations of the historic
district, Mumbai India, ± 2000.
photo: Rahul Mehrotra

Fig 5.4 idem

and market forces, Mehrotra has found another source: the players and rituals of the kinetic city, with its temporary but unstoppable presence on the streets of Mumbai. By developing design and other strategies that use the festive, the ritual and the temporary, he has paradoxically succeeded in having a lasting impact on the quality and usefullness of public space. Again, there is an implied megascale in Mehrotra's projects that is highly modernist in its ambition. To this day, cities like Mumbai are dominated not by the top-down planned objects and schemes of 'middle-of-the-road' planners, but by the seemingly unplanned and seemingly light presence of the informal, the semi-legal, the temporary and the ritual. For an ambitious planner-architect, who wants to get inside the urban control room, focussing on the kinetic city seems only logical.

Jeanne van Heeswijk, Vlaardingen

The first two examples might suggest that Ditch Urbanism is specifically bound up with Second and Third World conditions of informal urban growth. This would be a mistake, since it is attitudes and methods that these practices share, not contexts. This attitude is equally visible in the work of some First World practices, like that of the Italian architects' group Stalker, who took the mile-long housing block *Corviale* in Rome, a rundown Utopia dating from the 1970s modelled on Le Corbusier's *Unité*, as an object for study and regeneration from within. In San Francisco there is Public Architecture, an office led by architect John Peterson, which has adopted similar strategies for the preservation and design of small public spaces in the area South of Market, for instance.

In the Netherlands, Jeanne van Heeswijk has been practising her brand of urbanism for years. She is an internationally known Dutch visual artist, partly based in New York City. Her longest and maybe toughest project has been in Vlaardingen Westwijk, a working-class community near Rotterdam built according to a High Modernist ideological scheme by the Dutch CIAM-affiliated urban planner Wim van Tijen in the 1950s.[4] What is happening to Westwijk now is happening to most similar projects not only in the Netherlands but also in France, Germany, and even the United States. A whole generation of city fabric, designed and built to the dictates of Modernist urban planning is being demolished and replaced by new housing stock. This has resulted in more private ownership and parking facilities and less social housing, high-rise, and public green space.

Van Heeswijk uses her 'innocence' as a visual artist to implement an entirely different urbanistic morality and vision. Under the guise of a community arts project leader, she immersed herself in Westwijk by setting up office in the area for three years, getting to know every inch of this economically poor but culturally rich community. She then convinced the housing corporation that owns most of the neighbourhood to lend her the dilapidated shopping centre for the period before its demolition. Displaying a guerilla-like resourcefulness, she turned the shopping centre into a cultural and arts, as well as social, centre. She played simultaneously on different levels, energizing the local inhabitants but also convincing the stately *Boijmans Van Beuningen Museum* of Rotterdam to use the shopping centre as a temporary auxiliary museum, organizing local handicrafts fairs but also inviting internationally renowned architects, artists, and thinkers to visit and work. She even managed to reanimate the Modernist architecture of the Van Tijen era by painting the whole structure fire engine red, establishing it as a hip urban centre. She worked 'bottom-up' with the community itself but combined this with 'top-down' cosmopolitan, sophisticated design, art, thinking, and entrepreneurship.

Starting as an innocent arts effort, the project became increasingly problematic because, with all the attention it attracted, it opened an un-welcome debate about how to treat Modernist high-rises. All the clichés about their anonymity, cultural poverty, ugliness, and economic hopelessness were proven wrong. The inhabitants became proud of their area and less inclined to follow top-down policies. Intellectuals from outside the neighbourhood were forced to see and understand these areas as not just abstractions. Jeanne van Heeswijk, with her deep immersion in local communities and virtuoso use of urban institutions and policies, is working similar to Urban Think Tank in Caracas and Rahul Mehrotra in Mumbai. Taking just one example of the tens of thousands of similar Modernist buildings from the fifties, and revealing its hidden potentials as a cultural motor, pinpoints the issue of whether this approach should perhaps have been tried everywhere where similar neighbourhoods have been surrendered and are now being demolished. If you can make it in Vlaardingen-Westwijk, you can surely make it anywhere. Accepting this means having to completely re-evaluate one of the most important urban notions and planning policies of the last decade: the hopelessness of Modernist housing developments. Van Heeswijk's highly elegant intervention carries an enormous, if indirect, urbanistic punch.

Unlike middle-of-the-road practices that conform to the organizational rules, Ditch Urbanists

Fig 5.5 'De Strip', Vlaardingen-Westwijk, 2002
photo: Jeanne van Heeswijk

are oppositional. They have to prove constantly that things can and should be done differently by different people with different goals. They have to keep their blueprints, visions, and ambitions tucked away – revealing them would blow their cover. They have to sneak in through the backdoor and create 'facts on the ground', so that when the powers-that-be recognize what is going on, it might be too late to stop them. Ariel Sharon, the architect of the Palestinian occupation, coined the phrase 'creating facts on the ground' in 1973 when talking about building so many Israeli settlements on the West Bank that a future withdrawal from the Arab territory would be very difficult for his own government to realize. 'Create new facts on the ground and your political opponents don't have to agree with your view of the world, they have to deal with it.'[5]

This brings to light a last element of the Ditch urbanism: it is different from bottom-up urbanism and advocacy planning; it does not passively translate the will of local people. It brings to sites a fresh view of the world, not just the one used by official policy-makers or market parties. That is what makes these practices modernist, echoing a belief in the emancipatory powers of the urban collective that ran through urban planning from Patrick Geddes and Ebenezer Howard, through Lewis Mumford and Clarence Stein, Ernst May and Cornelis van Eesteren, George Candilis, Constantinos Doxiadis and Jacqueline Tyrwhitt, Victor Gruen, and of course José Luis Sert. These modernists form a Diaspora of crown princes exiled by *faux avant-garde* academism and market-place conformism. Just when we think that some urban problems are too vast and complex to be addressed by urbanists, they will emerge from the ditch with their ideology intact and with a new arsenal of tools to provide our cities with a much needed visionary energy.

Fig 5.6 idem

– This article is an abridged version of an essay that appeared first in Harvard Design Magazine, autumn 2006, number 25.

NOTES

1   Neil Young, Liner Notes to Decade, Warner Bros. Records, 1977
2   A. Brillembourg, K. Feireiss, H. Klumpner (ed.), Informal City: Caracas Case, Prestel Verlag Munich–Berlin–New York, 2005
–   View also the website of the Urban Think Tank: www.u-tt.com
3   Rahul Mehrotra's website: www.rma-associates.com
4   M. Berendsen (ed.), De Strip 2002–2004 Westwijk Vlaardingen, Amsterdam 2004
–   Jeanne van Heeswijk's website: www.jeanneworks.net
5   rivertext.com/factsOn_3.html

The Future Belongs to a Nation That Builds: About the Landscape of the Netherlands.

ADRIAAN GEUZE

ESSAY 06
ARCHITECTURE BULLETIN Nº 02│2006

Adriaan Geuze (1960) is co-founder and director of the firm West 8 Urban Design & Landscape Architecture, in which connection he has been responsible for the urban plan for Borneo Sporenburg (Amsterdam), the design of the Schouwburgplein in Rotterdam, and the Buona Vista Park in Singapore. As the curator of the 2nd International Architecture Biennale, he argued strongly in favour of preserving the Dutch polders. Here Geuze sheds light on his standpoint in an interview with himself.

- **Does the furore caused by Dutch architecture extend to Dutch landscape architecture?**

We first have to acknowledge that architecture from countries such as Switzerland and Spain has also drawn a great deal of interest. The Netherlands is important in this international context, but certainly not unique. The remarkable thing about landscape architecture is that it primarily functions and evolves on the medium scale, the scale of the visual styling of streets and squares and the creation of suburban parks. The Netherlands is not a pioneer in this regard. However, in order to answer the question about the state of landscape architecture in the Netherlands, I must discuss our landscape. It is only when we broaden our gaze to see the larger scale that it becomes intriguing: the Netherlands is remarkable because of its man-made landscape. And not just that: the Dutch also think differently about nature. That obviously plays a part in how the landscape has evolved, and it is primarily this that stirs interest.

- **How important is the Dutch landscape?**

The landscape is the most distinctive and all-embracing cultural tradition of the Dutch nation. Compared with, for example, Russia, Ireland or Germany, we can safely say that it is not our literature or music that epitomizes our culture. The country has, of course, produced great masters in these artistic forms, but none of their oeuvres has encapsulated the Dutch universe or formed a fountainhead or benchmark for an extended period. For the art of painting it is quite a different story: Vermeer,

Rembrandt, Mondrian and countless other painters are the true visual standard-bearers of our culture.

The Dutch Masters are internationally regarded as icons of the Netherlands. They are what Shakespeare is for Great Britain, Bach and Goethe to Germany, and Tolstoy to Russia. If there is such a thing as a Dutch soul, then this is not revealed in words or music, but in pictures, in the oil paint on those innumerable canvases. And no form of artistic expression is as indebted to the country of polders as painting. Without polders there would have been no Rembrandt. It is no accident that the genre of landscape painting was invented here. The seventeenth-century masters were bowled over by the beauty of the land that had just been created. Their euphoria about this polder landscape radiates on the walls: the open plain – rectilinear and immense – the horizon and the low sky, the divine light with its broad colour spectrum, but also the grey desolation and mist. The painters were hypnotized by the way in which the sunlight caresses the perfectly level land, by the windmills, the livestock, and the water. Their nineteenth-century colleagues heightened the effect

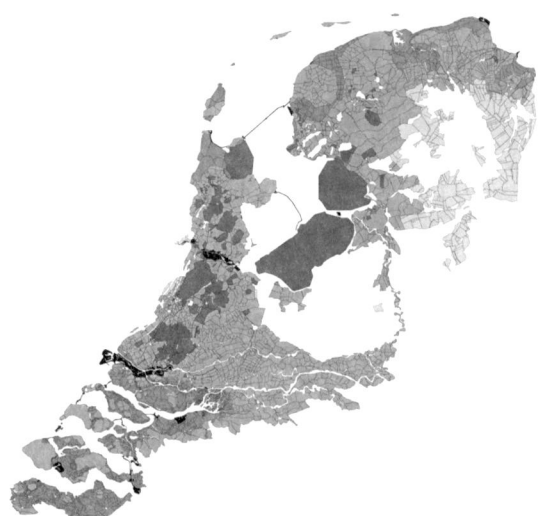

Fig 6.1   raclaimed land
image: MUST

even further, presenting the polder landscape as it could potentially be: supremely Arcadian or a miserable marshland.

- **You mean Van Gogh isn't a Dutchman?**

Not every great Dutch painter conforms to this viewpoint. Van Gogh, for example, did not originate from the polders and nor did he feel at home there. However, he did paint that polder landscape, in ash-grey and willow-grey tones. His windmill-filled landscape close by Dordrecht also tells a story about the polder: life's drabness there. It drove Van Gogh crazy. 'Homesickness is preferable to Holland,' wrote Leo Vroman – words that might have been penned for Van Gogh. Vincent van Gogh had little understanding of the Dutch landscape, having little affinity with the exceptional light and primarily seeing the mist. It was not until he reached the south of France that he could indulge his crazy colour blindness.

- **Aren't you exaggerating about those painters?**

Not at all. We must devote this much attention to painters if we are talking about the landscape, because painters – like photographers today – reveal to us how we have started to look, or might look, at our surroundings with new eyes. It is not just about the registration of the image, but about its power. A good example is the Paris of the nineteenth century, where the European metropolis as a phenomenon took shape and became visible. Here the artists created a homage to 'the city'. The city with its boulevards, cafés and prostitutes became the explicit subject for painters and photographers. In exactly the same way, landscape painting resulted in a new perspective of the world two centuries earlier.

Hobbema celebrated the new orthogonal landscape. With the limp, impotent sails of ships anchored in the roadstead, Albert Cuyp sublimated the becalmed wind and restlessness before the storm. Ruysdael was the king of the low sky, the towering clouds above the insignificant land. Potter showed us the horizon through the legs of the bull. Each in their own way, Rembrandt and Vermeer stole the light and made it sparkle and glow. Jongkind, Gabriël and Roelofs captured the soft, almost creamy grass, combed by the wind. Just like Don Quichote, they too had an obsession with windmills: those ever-present windmills, that restlessness of the sails, the diagonals in a land of lines – Mondrian and Van Doesburg even had arguments about them.

- **So what does that landscape represent for us?**

The landscape – in the way we look at it, represent it and have worked on it – has given us a great deal. It is possible to draw a direct line from the creation of land and the toil in the quagmire and on the seabed to our way of behaving. A culture that does all these things eventually falls under the spell of its own pragmatism. It sounds banal, but it is only with unashamed pragmatism that a country situated below sea level can survive.

With its razor-sharp horizon, the polder landscape razes every attempt to be superior. It enforces co-ordination and equality. Popes and dictators have no place in this country. With the sea pounding against them incessantly, raising dikes was only possible with a collective commitment and sacrifice. The land therefore requires an explicit positioning: are you contributing or are you excluded? The position inside or outside the dike is a constant issue. There must always be clarity; an avowal is required of everyone. Fundamental equality, the constant awareness of the threatening 'Flood' and the sacrifice it requires have resulted in the roots of Calvinism running deep here. Grandiosity and gloominess alternate here, like high tide and ebb, like sun and rain. Thomas Jefferson's grid, which served as a model of colonization based on equality for the West, is inextricably bound up

Fig 6.2   polder Schieveen / photo: Adriaan Geuze

Fig 6.3   Willem Roelofs, Polder at Abcoude ± 1870
image: Haags Gemeentemuseum

with the essence of the United States and the American Dream. The tradition of creating land is embedded in the DNA of the Dutch in a similar way. The polder landscape is the resulting product.

- **So the polder landscape is central?**

The polder landscape is so central that, since the 1930s, a succession of planners have taken the realization of a representative metropolis specific to the Netherlands for granted: the so-called Randstad, or 'Rim City'. This metropolis, with the magical polder landscape of Holland as its empty centre, was internationally regarded as attractive and pioneering: the perfect dialogue between city and landscape! The city-dweller cycles and skates from his front door to the cows. For his or her daily dose of fresh air, this urbanite

Fig 6.4 polder Schieveen
photo: Adriaan Geuze

traverses the landscape that is reborn from the mist every morning ... for free. Sunsets and horizontal rain accompany the changing of the seasons. The city-dweller enjoys the benefit of the urban facilities as well as the centuries-old history of the land in all its stratification. As with Istanbul and the Bosporus or in Rio and Manhattan, the linkage between a metropolis and its natural setting was the main issue. That Randstad, which was to be the apotheosis of the polder landscape, is history. The dreamed-of metropolis with its direct connection to the landscape would not be realized.

- **But what about the Netherlands now?**
I am unaware of any instances of 'land creation'.
Anyone who looks at the Netherlands now cannot fail to be concerned. The draining of land to create polders has come to a standstill, and there is no modern-day example of land creation. Nobody is staking a claim to the future, even though it has never been so simple and cheap. The North Sea is a shallow sea above an immense quantity of sand – here lies a whole Sahara! The fleet of suction dredgers that is creating the Palm Islands in the Persian Gulf or has raised Hong Kong's airport could, in a spare moment, double the surface area of the Netherlands. The future belongs to a nation that builds[1]: there is an unavoidable parallel between the Dutch Golden Age and the ambitious projects for land reclamation. In other words, the periods when we were focused on other affairs and there was no land reclamation activity coincide with periods of cultural stagnation and regression. As the most densely populated country in Europe, it is extraordinary that we now seem to be renouncing our tradition of land reclamation. How can the Netherlands, especially at this point in time, when everyone is desperate for space – space to live, space for nature, space for economic activity – abandon land reclamation? Why is that not a political issue?

Not only are we allowing our tradition to be watered down, but I also notice that we have acquired a well-nigh perverse appetite for demolishing and fragmenting the mighty polder landscape, the landscape that was so painstakingly formed and cherished by previous generations. I am not referring to Southern Flevoland, where Almere is expanding as rapidly as any Asian city into an affordable alternative for the woodland residential setting of Het Gooi. Nor am I referring to the Port of Rotterdam, which has staked a claim to the future by planning out its expansion into the Maasvlakte 2 port and industrial zone. No, I am referring to the two-dimensional metropolis that is currently taking shape in our country, in a way similar to how Los Angeles has developed. As in this desert city, the citizen has no relationship with the landscape, and history – just like the flexibility – has disappeared.

This two-dimensional metropolis amounts to the construction of a suburban prison that is marketed under the theme of 'innocence', a theme that succeeds in attracting families with children. As in Los Angeles, people find their bearings using motorway exits. The tailback corridors are separated from the polder landscape by sound barriers, greenhouses, and warehouses. The latest railway link to be constructed actually dives beneath it. The only features of the polder landscape that seem able to play a role in this new, poorly organized network are the numerous original waterside cities. These are the historical anchor, the link with the past.

The promise of the phenomenal international city that could be developed between Schiphol Airport and the ArenA stadium, as our version of Hong Kong or Singapore, is hampered and held in check at almost every turn. After all, the political preference seems to lie with the dreary élan of the succession of highway exits from Breukelen all the way to Zwolle, Veenendaal and Goes. 'The future belongs to a nation that builds,' is a claim that rings from every municipal councillor's lips. There are indeed projects that look ahead to a New Netherlands, but their scope is largely regional and they primarily involve reorientations within the existing landscape: the Wieringerrandmeer project to re-flood a polder, the Blauwe Stad ('Blue City', an 800-hectare residential and recreational development amidst re-flooded polders to the east of Groningen), and the Grensmaas (the 'Border Meuse' flood prevention project that creates space for the River Meuse's channel and forelands along the Dutch-Belgian border), to name but a few. Among the Vinex plans, it is chiefly the IJ-oevers (Banks of the IJ) and the IJ-brug (the IJburg Bridge leading to Amsterdam's ambitious expansion area) that have proven innovative. The other plans are often nothing more than short-term concepts for suburban living, usually in low-lying polders.

- **If we take stock of the current situation, is the outlook then so gloomy?**

Yes, the Netherlands clearly believes it can allow itself the liberty of wiping out its own cultural heritage. Instead of this, people could employ the collective talent for the creation of new land that provides space and new economic perspectives. A fixation on nothing more than the supposed 'market' – illogical for the Netherlands – means that we will end up living in a country for frightened refugees. Consumers have no desire to identify themselves with immigrants in cities and actually deliberately avoid them. They seek their 'housing product' in alarmingly low-lying polders because of the apparent lack of alternatives. The National Spatial Strategy, the magnum opus of the baby-boom generation, gives no priority to alternatives. This act places the procedure above the vision and, by definition, leaves no room for figures like Berlage, Lely, or J.P. Thijsse: people with blueprints and visionary ideas. The Spatial Planning of the Netherlands has no idea how to handle new infrastructure, land reclamation, airports, higher dikes, large expanses of nature, and so on. The abandonment of clear-cut lines on the planning maps has given rise to a situation in which every acre of Dutch land that could possibly be developed has essentially become an object of speculation. Dutch agriculture, once world-renowned, cannot survive here. This has resulted in a gloomy vicious circle: land is too expensive, so the agriculture disappears, and the land can then be developed. The Dutch tradition, our pleasure in creating land, has disappeared. The Dutch landscape is facing a serious crisis.

NOTE

I Freely after Cornelis Lely's quote: "a living nation builds for its future" (to be found on the monument on the "Afsluitdijk", the dike that closed the Zuyder Sea).

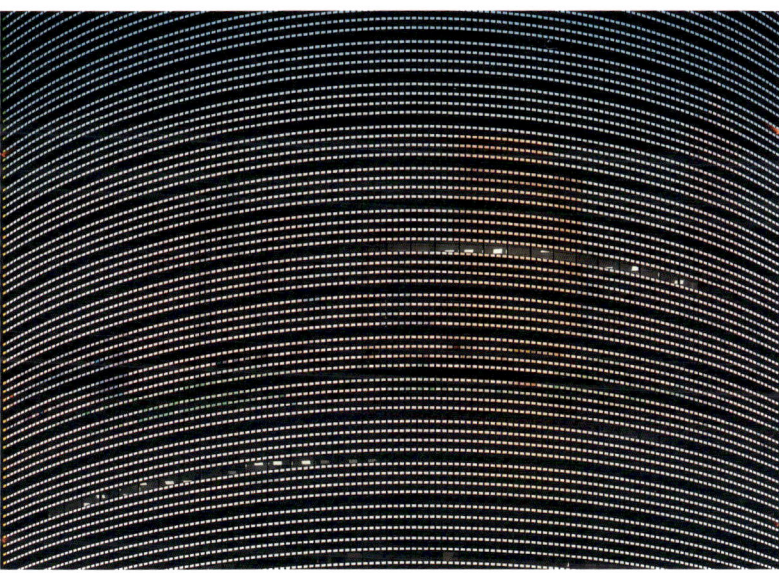

Eurocentrism

The One-Sided History of European Architecture

HANS IBELINGS

Hans Ibelings (1963) is an art historian and the editor-in-chief of AIO NEW EUROPEAN ARCHITECTURE. He has authored a number of books on contemporary architecture, among them SUPERMODERNISM: ARCHITECTURE IN THE AGE OF GLOBALIZATION. Soon to appear is his book EXPLORING EUROPE: ARCHITECTURE IN THE 21ST CENTURY; this essay is a prepublication of the first chapter.

Every history is a construction. In the case of the history of architecture it is an undeniably Eurocentric construction. The view of the architectural history rendered by most general surveys revolves around two millenniums in Europe, with North America taking a share in the story only from the nineteenth century onwards, and with Japan and Latin America appearing only in the mid twentieth century – the latter playing little more than a walk-on part as a representative of tropical modernism. That is at least more substantial than the trivial roles set aside for the rest of Asia, Africa and Australia even to this day. Eurocentrism in architectural history is less than desirable, and it is significant that several efforts to write a globally more equitable history have been undertaken in recent years. At the same time, we must frankly admit the existence of a connection between the architectural Eurocentrism that emanates from the history books, the Western conception of art and architecture history, and the relatively high concentration of architecture in Europe. It is precisely because of this connection that the writing of

architectural history has been able to uphold such a Eurocentric stance. The large volume of historical research that has been, and is being, undertaken on European architecture serves only to buttress this position. Most histories of architecture thus still remain accounts of architecture in Europe, even when the word 'Europe' or 'European' is absent from the title of the book concerned.

Consider Kenneth Frampton's 1980 book *Modern Architecture: A Critical History* in which the choice of subject matter is far from atypical for the genre of general surveys. India receives attention only for the work carried out there by Lutyens and Le Corbusier, Japan only for Metabolism, and Latin America only for tropical modernism. The geographical scope of Frampton's book differs little, for example, from that of *Storia dell'architettura moderna* by Leonardo Benevolo published twenty years earlier, or from the short review of modern architecture by William Curtis which appeared not long after Frampton's. Of the 27 chapters in the second part which forms the bulk of Frampton's book, five and one quarter are about American architecture. The rest is about Europe, and apart from a chapter and a half on the Soviet Union, it concentrates exclusively on Western Europe, without any explanation from Frampton of why he adopts such stringent geographical limits.

The image that rises from Curtis's 1982 book *Modern Architecture Since* 1900 is a touch more indulgent. Besides the usual Eurocentrism, one chapter is at least devoted to 'Modern Architecture and Developing Countries Since 1960'. The opening sentences of that chapter make it clear why in the author's view the history of modern architecture is at heart a European one, or by extension a Western one: 'Modern architecture was created in industrialized countries where a progressivist world view flourished temporarily, and where avant-garde cliques attempted to produce an authentic modern style appropriate to rapidly changing social conditions. This curious pattern was not repeated elsewhere, but its results were copied all around the world, and were often misapplied.' That was apparently sufficient reason to devote just one chapter to the subject. (Curtis, 1992, p.356)

The second edition of Curtis's book, issued in 1987, contains an addendum to that single chapter under the title 'The Search for Substance: Recent World Architecture', which is again not purely Eurocentric and which touches on recent architecture in the Middle East, among other things. This changes little, however, of the essence of Curtis's interpretation of modern architecture as a Western concept. His argument may be regarded as a restrained version of the approach Nikolaus Pevsner had taken forty years earlier in *An Outline of European Architecture*, which appeared in 1943. In his preface to the revised edition of 1960, Pevsner stated that 'Western' and 'European' were synonymous as far as he was concerned, and that these words had a definition that was not so much geographical as cultural. In Pevsner's view, the western boundary of Europe did not stop at the Atlantic Ocean: American architecture puts in an appearance in the final chapter, and in later additions there is even an American Postscript that discusses both North American and Latin American examples. Nor did he locate the eastern border of Europe at the Bosporus or the Urals. Pevsner's Europe halts at the eastern frontier of the Western Roman Empire, or, in the revised preface of 1960, at the then so predominant Iron Curtain. He systematically omitted anything to the east of that border. In explanation, Pevsner adduced the example of Bulgaria: 'If it is never mentioned at all in the following pages the reason is that Bulgaria in the past belonged to the Byzantine and then to the Russian orbit, and that her importance now is so marginal as to make her omission pardonable.' (Pevsner, 1990, p.10)

Henry-Russel Hitchcock's *Architecture: Nineteenth and Twentieth Centuries*, originally published in 1958, followed a similar Eurocentric pattern, except that it registered developments in the United States from the early nineteenth century onwards which in the author's view formed part of Western architecture. He discussed American architecture not only in separate chapters, but also integrated it into his descriptions of the development of architecture in Europe. More clearly than anyone else, he articulated the viewpoint that American architecture is inseparable from that of Europe: because several prominent architects such as Henri Hobson Richardson or Richard Morris Hunt trained in Paris, for example, because British architecture journals were the main source of information, and, not least, because European modernists ranging from Schindler and Neutra to Mies Van de Rohe and Walter Gropius had emigrated to the US. Hitchcock, moreover, had an obvious appreciation and esteem for the specifically American contribution to Western architecture, such as the work of Sullivan and Wright, the development of the skyscraper, and the apotheosis of modernism in the American work of Mies van der Rohe. In the final chapter of his book, 'Architecture at the Mid Century', Hitchcock noted that the 'Western world' had become 'enormously larger in geographical extent' by around 1950 and now included not only Western Europe and North America but Latin America and even Japan (but mentioning the last of these only in passing without going into a specific architect or architecture).

In the Epilogue added to a later edition of the book in 1971, Hitchcock discussed the new situation in which Western architecture was no longer the exclusive domain of Western Europe and the US, prompting a rhetorical question: 'So far Eastern Europe, Asia, and Africa have, on the whole, been learners and disciples of the West. Will the countries of Eastern Europe, and the new countries of Asia and Africa soon be making contributions towards a new world-style, such as in the last few decades first the North Americans, next the Latin Americans and then the Japanese made? Will the history of Western European architecture continue to be the principle story (which thanks to the political conditions has been largely true up to the present) or will the Western European tradition (...) become in the succeeding period somewhat peripheral and even alien to a situation in which underdeveloped countries will increasingly, as they come of age, tend to throw off cultural tutelage as they have mostly already thrown off political control?' (Hitchcock, , 1987, p.591)

Judging from later-written books, in which Hitchcock's present and imminent future have already turned into history, the answer must be negative. Most architectural histories still treat architecture as implicitly Western, Western architecture as primarily European, and European architecture specifically Western European. And they do not do so without reason. Classical architecture did indeed begin in Greece, but by the time of the Roman Empire it had developed into a European architecture. Since then practically all the movements and styles that fill the textbooks have had their roots in the western part of Europe. For Romanesque architecture, these lay in Italy and France, while the Gothic originated in Île de France; the Renaissance started in Italy, as did the baroque which also had roots in Austria, Prussia and Bohemia; neoclassicism originated in England and France, and modern architecture in Germany, France, the Netherlands and the Soviet Union. The last of these countries is the only exception to the rule that everything comes from the West. Apart from that, Eastern Europe scarcely figures. This narrowness applies not only to Poland, Hungary, Romania and the Balkans, but similarly to Portugal, Spain, Sweden and Finland – countries that crop up only incidentally when some famous individual has worked there, such as Álvaro Siza, Antoni Gaudí, Gunnar Asplund or Alvar Aalto. It is evident enough that architectural history as usually written is largely dominated by European architecture and a European outlook on architecture. But that the definition of what constitutes European architecture is so narrow, and that it is constrained to a limited area of Western Europe is striking, to put it mildly.

Pevsner was not the only author to justify the omission of Eastern Europe by the curious argument that it did not belong to the West and had moreover failed to produce anything of importance. The categorical exclusion of practically the whole of

Central and Eastern Europe as well as all countries on the periphery of Western Europe, is characteristic of all the standard works of the last fifty years. It may give the appearance of an opinion founded on secure knowledge (as exemplified by Pevsner's comment on Bulgaria) but that appearance is questionable. That the opinion is an outcome of a lack of knowledge is more plausible. Since we seldom hear anything about Bulgaria, at least in any language familiar to Western European ears, we take it for granted that there is nothing going on there that is worth mentioning. In place of Bulgaria, you could substitute the name of any other East European country, Portugal, Norway or Ireland. While I am prepared to believe that there has been no Bulgarian Le Corbusier, it is surely highly improbable, given the statistical observation that creative talent is more or less uniformly distributed, that Bulgaria has not brought forth a single architect worthy of note.

The lack of knowledge may be at least partly explained as a heritage of the Cold War, which did not make it at all easy to acquire insight from within the bulwarks of Eurocentric architectural history into what was happening in architecture or architectural history in Eastern Europe. The sole exception to this was formed by the avant-gardes of Soviet architecture, about whom much was published, not only in the Soviet Union itself but in Western Europe and the United States, notably during the seventies. Whatever had happened or was going on in architectural respects elsewhere in Eastern Europe was long hard to discern and hence treated as non-existent, despite various attempts to at least summarize developments there, such as the effort by G.E. Kidder Smith, who dedicated a short chapter to Eastern Europe in *The New Architecture of Europe; An Illustrated Guide Book and Appraisal*, first published in 1961. His personal contacts and his efforts to acquaint himself with architecture journals published in the Eastern Bloc enabled him to conclude his book with a concise but informative 'Note on Eastern Europe', where he noted some encouraging prospects. One of the few other authors who has retained an eye for Central and Eastern Europe has been Udo Kultermann, who has surpassed anyone else in seeking means to break open the Eurocentric writing of history in books such as *New Directions in African Architecture*, *New Ar-*

chitecture in the World and *Zeitgenossische Architektur in Osteuropa* published in 1980.

The works of Kultermann and Kidder Smith still count as anomalies in architectural history, however. In quantitative respects they are certainly no match for the endless stream of publications that peer no farther eastwards than Prague, Vienna or Budapest. Perhaps contrary to what one might expect, the dissolution of the Iron Curtain has changed this situation only to a minor degree. Seventeen years after the fall of the Berlin Wall, the cultural dividing line has in no way disappeared, and a huge gulf continues to yawn between the knowledge about the East and the West, a gulf which is preserved purely by the positive feedback mechanism that infuses every art historical discipline. Reiterating what predecessors have already written automatically makes whatever is regarded as important even more important, etching the well-trodden paths ever-deeper so that it becomes increasingly difficult to deviate from them. The significance of Western European architecture has already been described so exhaustively and repetitively, and will no doubt continue to be so ad infinitum, that little room is left for other interpretations.

It seems that the partition of Europe during the Cold War years has drawn an opaque veil over the totally different geopolitical patterns that existed in Europe before then. It is typical of the standard works that terms like the Habsburg Empire are rarely mentioned and the present names of the nations concerned are always used, resulting for example in a neglect of Austria's connections with Central Europe and the Balkans.

Moreover, the difference in the extent and quality of that knowledge continues to exist because the international book market is still dominated by West-European publishers. This, too, contributes to a preservation of the imbalance. Anyone who dips into a Czechoslovakian book on twentieth century architecture – such as Felix Haas's 1978 book *Architektura 20. Století; Státní pedagogické nakladatelství*, for example – will generally encounter all those buildings that matter in the West, plus the highlights of Central and Eastern Europe. The converse is never true.

The asymmetrical attention paid to different parts of Europe may of course be considered a justifiable reflection of the fact that Bulgaria (to take that same example again) has failed to produce any figures of the stature of Hans Scharoun or Jean Nouvel, while Germany and France have done so. But whether someone becomes a celebrity is not solely a question of personality and talent, but also of the circumstances under which the talent concerned has had the opportunity to develop such prominence. The way history is written down is irrefutably one of those circumstances, and for many reasons it has been more favourable in Western Europe than elsewhere. In a reunited Europe, in an era of globalization, when information can be exchanged so much more quickly and effortlessly so that the contrast between the centre and the periphery becomes ever smaller and less relevant, there are healthy prospects that something will change in this situation. The circumstances for such change are now better than ever, all the more so because, nearly twenty years after the disappearance of the biggest political barrier that recently divided Europe, the level of cultural exchange has become more intense than ever. Given the presumption that the way architectural history is written is to some extent influenced by developments in contemporary architecture, it may be expected that the rising interest in what is going on outside the West European centres, and in particular in the eastern part of the Continent, will soon have the effect of sharpening the historiographic focus on those regions.

Whether that will be sufficient to radically change the construction of the history of architecture is dubious, which is not to say impossible. The process of erosion, the outcome of positive feedback, has already gone too far for that: practically every book portrays a past consisting of an identical succession of undisputed masterpieces and crowning achievements by an all-star team of architects from all periods. Nonetheless, there is more prospect than ever that the well-worn paths of this Eurocentric history may be enriched with knowledge of what has been taking place in the supposedly unimportant parts of Europe, of the developments in the peripheral zones. That could lead (although theoretical standpoints may be getting entwined with optimistic speculation here) to a shift of perspective in European architecture history, and perhaps, hopefully, to a change from what presently appears to be an inviolably monolithic

West-European construction into a more heterogeneous pan-European construction.

— This is a prepublication from *Exploring Europe; Architecture in the 21st Century*, to be published by NAI Publishers in collaboration with A10 New European Architecture.

RESOURCES:

- Benevolo, L., Storia dell'architettura moderna, Roma, Laterza, 1987.
- Curtis, W.J.R., Modern Architecture since 1900, Oxford, Phaidon, 1992 (1982/1987).
- Frampton, K., Modern Architecture: a critica History, London, Thames and Hudson, 1980.
- Haas, F., Architektura 20. Století, Praha, SPN (Státní pedagogické nakladatelství), 1978.
- Hitchcock, H.R., Architecture: Nineteenth and Twentieth Centuries, Harmondsworth, Penguin Books, 1987 (1958/1971).
- Kidder Smith, G.E., The new Architecture of Europe, London, Prentice-Hall Int., 1961.
- Kultermann, U., New Directions in African Architecture, London, Studio Vista, 1969.
- Kultermann, U. (ed.), New Architecture in the World, London, Barrie and Jenkins, 1976.
- Kultermann, U., Zeitgenössische Architektur in Osteuropa, Köln, DuMont, 1985.
- Pevsner, N. (ed.), An outline of European architecture, Harmondsworth, Penguin Books, 1990 (1943/1960).

Calling a Halt to Deference

A Plea for Curiosity

WINY MAAS

ESSAY 08

ARCHITECTURE BULLETIN N° O2 | 2006

Winy Maas (1959) formed the architecture practice MVRDV together with Jacob van Rijs and Nathalie de Vries in 1991. With its experimental research project and dazzling designs, MVRDV has established a strong position for itself in international architecture. In this monologue, written up by art historian Mieke Dings, Maas calls for an end to the suffocating climate that has gripped Dutch architecture in the twenty-first century.

"In Dutch architecture the shocks of 9/11 and of the assassinations of Pim Fortuyn and Theo van Gogh have brought about a trend towards traditionalism and an old-fashioned notion of craft. This has meant that the experimental culture shaped by the 1990s architects (including MVRDV) is largely in danger of extinction. These architects have therefore sought their fortune farther from home, and Holland's reputation as an exciting country for architecture has begun to show signs of crumbling. A feeling of foreboding became general, and traditionalist architecture was deployed to reassure us. A new curiosity about ideas and activities in other countries and the instigation of new research are needed if we are to wake from this state of hibernation and again become leaders in the theater of international architecture. The Netherlands Architecture Institute (the NAI), the Delft School of Design, the Berlage Institute and the Netherlands Institute for Spatial Research can play a crucial role here.

It is interesting that Aaron Betsky was appointed director of the NAI at the point when Dutch architecture had attained a peak of optimism, and that he was very soon confronted with a total reversal of that situation, with gloom taking the foreground. Attracted by the flourishing climate for architecture in the 1990s and realizing that this made Holland unique, Betsky has constantly attempted to preserve something of this passion for renewal. In the 1990s the generation labeled as 'SuperDutch' by Bart Lootsma in 2000 and which represented a second wave of modernism in Holland was given every opportunity to develop. The expanding economy and steadily rising property prices created a climate in which many clients wanted interesting architecture as a feather in their caps, and this in turn led to increased demand. The prospect of further European unification boosted the desire for difference still more. In that regard Holland too had to do something to catch up with the other European capitals, where the quest for a typical urban architecture had begun much earlier. One of the strong points then was that Holland was prepared to welcome knowledge and expertise from abroad and did not carry on like the sad cartoon dicky-bird Calimero ("It's unfair. They are big and I am small"). Concurrently with this openness to innovation, moreover, a cultural network was set up, with the Netherlands Architecture Institute (1988), the Netherlands Architecture Fund (1993) and the Mondriaan Foundation (1994), which also offered architects and critics the financial leverage to embark on research and explore their field at greater depth. Various architecture prizes were set up at the same time, such as the NAI Prize for young architects (which MVRDV won in 2002, the first year it was awarded), and the Bronze Beaver, for inspirational clientship (founded in 1989).

This optimistic climate, favorable to innovation and in-depth exploration, offered young architects plenty of opportunities. The generation that was trained during the 1980s had rejected the somewhat dreary sense of

Fig 8.1   Design Pig City 2001
image: MVRDV

Fig 8.2   Frøsilos Copenhagen,
Denmark 2005
photo: Rob het Hart

commitment of the decade before and was aided and abetted by the self-confidence and intelligent, critical approach of Rem Koolhaas. When Jacob van Rijs, Nathalie de Vries and I founded MVRDV in 1991, Holland was totally preoccupied with making room for the American intellectualism of Peter Eisenman and his friends. Dutch architects felt somewhat intimidated by their complicated statements about the symbolic value of architecture, which were often totally incomprehensible for outsiders. Meanwhile however it also became plain that this theoretical design approach did not lead to many actual commissions. On the other hand there was the intellectualism of the French School, including Paul Virilio, whose texts about the influence of speed on various aspects of society was obligatory reading, although they often left us confused however about how to translate them into architecture. Architects like Herman Hertzberger, Aldo van Eyck and Rem Koolhaas offered reference points for the quest for an alternative approach and challenged us to provide a proper response to intellectualism.

MVRDV opted then for a scientific attitude to design. By means of *datascaping*, a term that has by now become more common property but which was innovatory at the time, we mapped the forces at play and the requirements involved with each assignment, so as to come up with a whole gamut of possibilities. Later we expanded this method into scenario planning, by which the consequences of every decision were rendered visible immediately. Crucial to devising this methodology, which as we see it forms part of a long Dutch tradition of investigative urban planning, was the innovatory spirit of the booming nineties. It offered the intellectual and financial space to explore the limits of various environmental questions, such as that of urban density in *Farmax* (1998). But experiments were possible outside this conceptual field of research as well – with new materials, innovative typologies and unheard-of forms. There was such an optimistic mood, such curiosity, in Holland and as architects we were there to give visual form to that feeling. We did so, moreover, with an enthusiasm that was so infectious that in the mid-1990s Peter Buchanan wondered out loud whether Dutch modernist architecture wasn't heralding a new, global epoch, or whether it was just the last glory of the dying day – 'a sunset effect, a terminal exaggeration of aspects of modernism'.[1]

The new generation quickly got a name for its poetic pragmatism, its freshness, irony and candor. The press saw a link with the sobriety of the Dutch Golden Age, the tradition in Dutch civil engineering, of social engineering, the humanism of the peak years of *Nieuwe Bouwen*. Through joint excursions abroad, publications and group exhibitions we gradually acquired the trademark of being a "Dutch School". And while that sometimes felt very claustrophobic, it has contributed to a large degree to the great interest abroad in Dutch architecture. The NAI too has put "Dutch Design", this intriguing combination of architecture and design, on the map as an export product. That had already happened in the 1990s, but was reinforced by the keen observational technique that Aaron Betsky exhibited in various publications.[2] The interest abroad grew ever greater: architectural tourists dropped in on the SuperDutch projects and expressed their amazement about the fact that even new firms were given so many opportunities to build in Holland, while we were already sitting round the table less and less with the Dutch and more and more with Danes or Germans and later on even with Asians. In

the meantime Holland remained our exciting and challenging headquarters, where our designs played an ever greater role in political debate and the public arena. A good example is "Pig City" (2001), the tower block that in one blow solves the space problem of industrial pig farming, thus touching on a sensitive political and economic nerve and which had just been raised by Pim Fortuyn and other parties in their campaign programs for the 2002 election. Interesting times were a-coming.

9/11 and the assassination of Fortuyn changed the picture completely – the economy and social engineering were no longer key concepts; instead the political debate focused on moral values. In the world of architecture the new uncertainty was immediately apparent – a number of commissions didn't happen – in our case, the Arnhem-Nijmegen Technical High School (1998-2002) – and most of the projects planned before the bubble burst proved failures. Expensive urban projects and infrastructural plans were scrapped and architecture became cruder. The most distressing and significant result however was the ideological decline: while two generations of politicians debated issues in an atmosphere of impotence and doubt, in architecture too a desperate battle of directions was waged. Experiment and irony surrendered to a more traditional style. Crucial projects in Holland were suddenly being given to reassuring retro-architects like Kollhoff, Krier and their imitators. The Dutch architectural climate ceased to be dominated by curiosity about the future and displayed instead a tedious nostalgia for the past. At the same time the traditional craft aspect of architecture was embraced in a way which insinuated that it had completely vanished in the preceding period. It was forgotten that the experiments with ground plans, materials and concepts of the SuperDutch generation was also craft-oriented. Where our generation however made the choice of investing limited architectural budgets in concepts, the next one opted for far more expensive finishes and detailing. It is distressing that this came along with a fierce reaction against the conceptual side of SuperDutch architecture. Sjoerd Soeters circulated his view that the development of concepts stands in the way of an architect making good, functional and beautiful buildings. In the press this standpoint was regularly adopted and critics like Bernard Hulsman referred more than once to the supposed uninhabitable character of "blobs" and hyper-modernist buildings. The new order seemed to be saying, "how could we ever have let this happen?" Criticism followed market demand, which had also shifted in the direction of traditional architecture. Furthermore a commercialized version of the architecture of the 1990s sur-

faced, especially with office and company buildings, adopting the formal idiom but not the route that led to it. Debate in Holland became pronouncedly anti-conceptual and the methodologies developed during the 1990s – the cultivation of a scientific approach, the critical and enquiring stance, the transparency and immediacy – were dispensed with. One criticism of our firm was that our enthusiasm for digital methods has led us to pay too little attention to the artistic and intuitive side of architecture. The pendulum had just swung the other way. Where we, with our rational and research-based attitude, were reacting to an excessively 'artistic approach' that had led in the 1990s to quasi-autonomous buildings which showed no concern for the city plan as a whole, today voices are again being raised calling for architectural autonomy. In our view, it is always advantageous to come up with a comprehensible methodology, especially for larger-scale developments. In doing so we link up with the tradition of planners such as Van Lohuizen. And that brings us to another issue the critics pointed to – that we work at such a large scale. It is a criticism that has if anything encouraged us. It is our firm

Fig 8.3   Matsudai, Japan 2003
photo: Rob het Hart

Mirador, Madrid Spain 2004   Fig 8.4
photo: Rob het Hart

conviction that, in a country like Holland where social engineering has always been a crucial theme, an architect is absolutely obliged to think on this level. It is the only way to incorporate collective elements such as infrastructure, public space and national parks. "The sky's the limit" – that's how we see it. One illustration is our study with the European Space Agency (ESA) where we worked on the exploitation of satellite systems for related planning questions in the area of energy and climate management. That does not mean that the smaller scale has become less important for us: bottom-up and top-down must go together. That is why we designed the "RegionMaker" later on, a piece of software that combines both levels.

What the criticism we received has mostly done is to sharpen our approach. We regard communication and discussion as an essential part of our design practice – these are means of detecting "holes" in our thinking, of expanding our knowledge and generating, incorporating and responding to criticism, in the same way as our generation previously responded to French and Eastern-seaboard American intellectualism. A methodology like this would seem fundamentally lacking in present-day traditionalism.

A sort of *Berufsverbot* seemed to have been imposed on some of us. Real discussions, such as were badly needed at precisely that moment, were thus ruled out altogether. With all the attention going to building according to traditional methods, there was no room for the critical self-reflection needed to come up with intelligent responses. Many new firms were wiped off the map with the stroke of a pen and things were made difficult for the entire SuperDutch generation on their own national home turf.

The reversal in the climate forced us to look more to abroad for work, where the Dutch approach we had developed over the past years was recognized and appreciated. At the time we realized our pavilion for the Expo in Hanover (2000) it was seen as setting the trend for the Dutch experimentalist passion and faith in social engineering. Only a year later however it was no longer seen as representing the Dutch spirit, although ironically it brought us plenty of commissions abroad. In no time at all ninety percent of our commissions came from foreign countries. Dutch flexibility and poetic

Fig 8.5   design City Sofa,
Busan South-Korea 2005
image: MVRDV

design Liuzhou, Fig 8.6
Liuzhou China 2006
image: MVRDV

pragmatism made Dutch firms ideally suited to eagerly emerging architectural regions that are however not all that wealthy. The Chinese market for instance is very interested in innovative concepts but disposes over too limited funds to erect buildings with an excess of detail. Firms like MVRDV also have the advantage of having developed a working approach of working in partnership with project management companies that see to the actual implementation and construction side of commissions. This has meant that we can concentrate on the research aspect. This organizational form was ideal for foreign commissions where it was essential to work in partnership with a local architect.

By now Asia in particular has welcomed Holland with open arms – the outsourcing of talented individuals such as Richard Hutten to Korea and Rem Koolhaas to China are well-known – while at home people are battening down the hatches against the rest of the world. Our current rigid rules make it difficult to take on people from outside the EU, even though employees who speak Chinese are essential to carry out commissions there and ensure that our Dutch firm continues to get commissions and is able

above all to develop them. Holland is losing its nerve and other countries are taking over from us. In China for instance a planning system is being developed that was previously found only in Holland. The curiosity and youthful daring that was so typical of Holland is currently alive and well in Spain. In comparison with other European countries, prices of land and property were recently still low there, so that everyone has started investing in Spain. A climate has been created there in which opportunities are available in every region for young architects. Typical of the fresh wind blowing through Spain, as I see it, is the fact that we were able to develop the Mirador in Madrid (2004), a version of traditional block building that has been tipped on its side, with the traditional patio as a "hole" and an open-air terrace in the facade. A country that permits such a wink and a nod towards tradition disposes over a healthy degree of self-criticism. Of course questions about security, fear and democracy also play a role in Spain, but people are ready to look for solutions in a constructive fashion. Countries like Spain are also unable to comprehend the radical transformation that has taken place in Holland –

Fig 8.7   Park Rand Building Amsterdam,
Realised end of 2006
photo: Rob het Hart

design interior Les Halles,   Fig 8.8
Paris 2004
image: MVRDV

the very country they all admired for its vigorous and transparent culture is now retreating into a fear-ridden, groggy state of hibernation, asking itself timidly whether it isn't too small to host an event like the Olympic Games.

This attitude is deadly for Dutch culture. It damages the perception of Holland that prevails abroad of openness and the passion for experiment which turned Dutch architecture into such a successful export product. If this country possessed an information economy at all, then it certainly did so in the field of architecture. But if we go on this way, in a few years time the busloads of architectural tourists will stop heading our way and the international publicity about Dutch architecture will decline even further. Furthermore we will run the risk of successful architects and designers actively choosing to emigrate.

This is why the time is now ripe, when both generations of architects are still active in Holland both in actual practice and in teaching and while they still retain their ties with the Dutch spirit, for new life to be breathed into architecture. This can occur on the one hand by reopening windows on the world

and embracing a whole range of fresh ideas and on the other by concentrating on specific Dutch themes for research. The ambitious apparatus we developed in the 1990s with the NAI, the Netherlands Architecture Fund, the Netherlands Institute for Spatial Research (2002), the Berlage Institute (1990) and recently also the Delft School of Design (2004) ought to make curiosity, debate and decisiveness a Dutch speciality once again. Just as it did under Betsky the past years, the NAI should go against the trend and continue to open its doors to experimental architecture from both home and abroad. The advisory role too that it has taken on with its presence in important debates, by seeking publicity and occupying positions in important bodies, must be maintained. Funding organizations and research bodies should also have the courage to put subjects for research with a high degree of urgency on the map – climate change, for instance, or the technology of landscape and city planning. Holland has always been good in dealing with urgent issues and should continue to pay attention to them. Furthermore there are of course a number of typically Dutch themes such as social engineering and landscape. Not only

Fig 8.9   WOZOCO, Amsterdam 1997
photo: Thijs Wolzak

design Omotesando, Tokyo, Japan 2006 Fig 8.10
image: MVRDV

should further research be done in these fields and books on them published – they also call for steps to be taken in reality and institutions to back them up.

Perhaps the slightly naïve, but no less beautiful exercises of the 1990s will then take on a more sustainable form. The downswing in Holland has forced the SuperDutch generation to become adult, and the conceptual methodology has perhaps needed to become more weighty and focused. The young bloods of that time have become more businesslike and established over the past years so as to be able to confront *corporate* architecture at a professional level. Betsky has always stressed the importance of this process of maturation. Now that we have succeeded in growing up, it is time to take the reactionary Dutch climate by the scruff of the neck. Architects can play a role here, by making a stand and also by unleashing debate in the educational world. Our own firm for instance has, with "Nederland Stad", proposed an alternative physical planning, in which the classical provinces are eliminated as planning levels and replaced by administrative entities concerned with a few major projects or ambitions. The idea is for this to replace the present facilitating tone one finds in planning, that leads to a progressively worsening and stifling sprawl. It is high time to talk about structural proposals such as these.

Betsky's departure from the NAI, that of Alejandro Zaera-Polo from the Berlage Institute and the founding of the Delft School of Design amount to a momentum that could herald the dawn of a new age. Will we be waving or drowning? In the coming years our self-awareness will have hopefully matured sufficiently through discussion and curiosity, that we will be able to disregard the question Buchanan raised at the apex of Dutch architecture in 1998: "Could it be then, that the very conditions that have made modernism so natural to the Netherlands, as well as the (modernistic, WM) attitudes that now condition architectural and urbanistic debate there, make it difficult for the country to participate in shaping a new paradigm in architecture?" After the years in which collapse and humiliation have threatened, perhaps we could start demonstrating that the opposite is the case.

NOTES

1 Peter Buchanan, 'Netherlands Now', A + U, no. 336, 1998, pp. 4-23, p. 5.
2 For instance, Aaron Betsky, Adam Eeuwens, False Flat. Why Dutch Design is So Good, London 2004.

5 Million
Senseo Crema Fans
Can't Be Wrong

TIMO DE RIJK

Essay 09

ARCHITECTURE BULLETIN N° 02|2006

Late summer 2004 witnessed the publication of Aaron Betsky's book *False Flat*, which analyses the nature of modernization among the Dutch in general and Dutch designers in particular. According to Betsky, the interesting designers have aligned themselves with a centuries-old introverted cultural tradition whose focus is often literally on the inner rather than the outside world. The Dutch designer shapes his reality to suit himself, resulting in a kind of hyper-realism that expands and modifies the existing world rather than pursuing distant, unreachable objectives.

When Betsky, who was initiated into the culture of the Netherlands at an early age but writes about it with the intellectual distance of a foreigner, announced his intention to publish a book on design in the Netherlands, he seemed the ideal author to tackle a critical text on the design culture that has now gained worldwide renown under the label 'Dutch Design'. The book's subtitle, 'Why Dutch Design Is So Good', promised not a paean of praise but an explanation for the evident fact that Dutch designs occupy a special and significant place in the design world at large. It seemed a foregone conclusion that *False Flat*

Timo de Rijk (1963) is a writer, programme maker and researcher in the field of design and design history. In 1998 he took his doctorate at Delft University of Technology with the thesis *Het Elektrische Huis* (The Electric House). He reviewed Aaron Betsky's book *False Flat: Why Dutch Design Is So Good* when it first came out two years ago. Now that the dust has settled, he takes a fresh look at the book.

would be welcomed with open arms by the whole Dutch design milieu.

But things were not to turn out that way at all. Seldom have I seen a book starting in such a promising position, with such a plum subject and dream author, and so beautifully produced, ending up in so much trouble. What was to have been the sure-fire triumphal march of a sorely-needed analysis clashed head on with a design world already arrayed, at least in Holland, in immovable ranks. The result was that despite *False Flat* being such a splendid book, it provoked a discussion that was mainly about the products it had left out. With *False Flat* in hand, let us attempt to expose those products, which were so strikingly omitted, to Betsky's characteristic critique, and at the same time let us examine the relevance of the juncture at which the book was written.

Millennial Visions

False Flat has now been out for barely two years, but it is extremely interesting to note that it was actually written in 2001. *False Flat* originated roughly in the period between 2000, the symbolic year of the future, and the aftermath of 9/11, the symbolic debacle of the undisputed future of the world. The year 2000 did not resemble the year 1000 in the least. The century leading up to 1000 AD was fraught with decline, Christian revelation, heavenly expectations, plague and death, but the year on the verge of the current millennium was a Utopian vacuum. And that was rather odd, for during a good part of the nineteenth century and practically the whole of the twentieth, the year 2000 was emblematic of a distant but quite palpable future. Depending on the prognosticator, there beckoned a rosy prospect of space travel, food-pills, teleportation, floor-to-ceiling TV screens, household nuclear power generators, or a workers' paradise. Only occasionally were these beguiling reveries contradicted by bleak dystopias, grim scenarios in which modern human civilization would be cast back to the Stone Age by a nuclear winter, a Simian takeover, or whatever. Countless manufacturers, particularly in the 1960s and 1970s, pounced on the mythic allure of the upcoming millennium to boost their product images. Philips launched the Video 2000 system, for example, while the Dutch rediscovered the pleasures of the health spa at Thermae 2000, went dancing at Disco 2000 or dreamed of City 2000. As a schoolboy I was proud to wear a fu-

turistic bright-yellow wristwatch labelled Velona 2000 (only years later did I discover that it was a house brand of the Dutch department store Vroom & Dreesman). But the closer we actually came to the year 2000, the more our belief in a stunning new world, a total break with the known past, ebbed away. The millennium year itself eventually fizzled out like a damp squib. I trust nobody got too excited about the future held out by the Christianity-inspired Pax Americana of those days – certainly not in retrospect.

Y2K

At most it was the notorious dot-com bubble, which reached its climax in the spring of 2000, which seemed to hint at a new world. The unexpectedness of its bursting led to a global cultural pessimism of a kind known from earlier technological novelties. As in the past with the train, car and television, it was now the digital highway that was hailed as the shortest road to universal moral and cultural degeneracy.

As much as the dot-com revolution was regarded elsewhere as the start of a new social and business paradigm (except in non-Western countries and France, of course), the Dutch response was lukewarm and apathetic. For example, opinion-pollster Maurice de Hond with his pioneering Newconomy internet investment venture was seen here as the Simple Simon of the World Wide Web.

It was mainly the digital faithful themselves who delivered the death blow to the web nirvana in the Netherlands. The birds of varying feather who had predicted that the Millennium Bug would cause planes to start dropping out of the sky, life support machines to freeze up and practically every piece of equipment containing a programmed chip to expire at precisely 0:00 hours on 1 January 2000, were exposed as charlatans or swindlers within minutes of midnight striking. The dismal nadir of this episode in the Netherlands consisted surely of the doom-drenched forecasts of our Y2K committee, led by of all people the former Philips saviour Jan Timmer, in the run up to 2000.

That same year, we also finally became aware of the lack of Utopian calibre in Dutch architecture. In a major German exhibition of futuristic visions in 20th-century architecture, Dutch architects were conspicuous by their absence. Even artistic and social dreamers like Henk Wijdeveld or Mart Stam were missing. The architecture critic Hans van Dijk, on the occasion of Rem Koolhaas's farewell as a professor at Delft University of Technology in 1992, may well have denounced modern Dutch architecture as a toothless and bloodless 'schoolmasters' modernism, but by 2000 the whole tradition of Utopian architecture and social engineering had become no more than a routine gesture of well-meant pedantry.

False Flat served as a final epilogue to this mentality; it explained the whole modern history of Dutch design, and in particular of Dutch architecture, in terms of that peculiarly Dutch brand of modernism – not a Utopia at all but a stark hyper-realism. The Canon of Modern Buildings in Rotterdam was now no longer one of futuristic statements but of illustrations of the Dutch aversion to grand classical gestures, of lines of sight, symmetry and exuberance.

Reality – but whose reality?

It was not so much the fault of the architects (let alone other designers) whose work was discussed in *False Flat* that the book caught so much flak. Without even reading the book, Holland's successful industrial designers immediately saw themselves as automatic opponents of Aaron Betsky. *False Flat* is not only a denial of classical, heroic modernism and a lavishly illustrated exposé of the shortcomings of much artistic Dutch design; it is also a book about the products that do not appear in it. Not one of those hundreds of illustrations in *False Flat* portrayed a product designed for a mass market, let alone one that was the pride of Dutch industry or Dutch industrial designers. In *False Flat* you will find neither a winner of the Dutch Design or Red Dot Awards, nor a cunning invention like the hinge at the heart of the clap skate, nor a commercial megasuccess like the Philishave or the Bugaboo stroller.

The central and most appealing idea of *False Flat* is, again, the conceptual character of Dutch designs that are forever reinventing the world by rearrangement and intensification, resulting in a new, attractive artificiality. That is at least true for both the national character of the Dutchman, according to Betsky, and for the character of the interesting Dutch Designers ranging from MVRDV to Hella Jongerius.

Still, if a universally shared mentality is responsible for engendering exciting art, architecture and design in one particular sector, a similar effect must surely also be evident in practically any other cultural manifestation. So can there be a modern Dutch spirit apparent in seventeenth-century Dutch paintings, and in Dutch graphic design and architecture of the late twentieth century, but none whatsoever in the industrial designs by the contemporaries – indeed, student classmates – of Jurgen Bey, Richard Hutten and Hella Jongerius?

While keeping the Betskian Dutchness idea in mind, let us nonetheless leaf through a number of successful or typical Dutch commercial products. After all, you can't analyse a situation or prove a case by ignoring alternatives. We'll start with a real classic: the electric sun-tan lamp. The esteemed reader no doubt realizes that this masterpiece of electrical engineering is perfectly adapted to the Dutch market. The predominantly German manufacturers, as well as the Dutch firms Philips and Inventum, originally marketed these devices in Europe as a health-giving or pseudo-medical substitute for natural sunlight. The international manufacturers gradually dropped their medical claims for the product, while it grew apace with the prosperity of the 1980s into a single and then double-sided sunbed. Nevertheless, the original low-priced sun lamps clung doggedly to their proud place in the Dutch household. Nowadays it is one of the last, if not the very last, purely regional products in the Philips catalogue. It is easy to see the sunray lamp as a final, authentic surrogate for a sun-drenched holiday, or as an ideal appliance for getting an all-over tan at home. An obvious question here is whether this artificial source of solar radiation is meant for the Calvinist who would never dream of dropping his pants at the beach, or for the cash-strapped consumer who nonetheless insists on being seen with a year-round tropical tan. A case of conspicuous irradiation? It's a hard profession, being a cultural observer.

Let's consider another example, and a more topical one at that. A recent market hit has been the Beertender, or, if you prefer, the PerfectDraft (you have to watch out as a mere writer because you can get sued over products like these). This is the ultimate demonstration that the Dutch design tradition no longer bears any trace of the presumed social engineering component, by which the designer contributes to the civilization of 'hoi polloi'. The home draft beer dispenser is, after all, a symptom of just how far the ladies and gentlemen of the design community nowadays are removed from what was once a sincere battle against public enemy number one, alcoholic inebriation. But the image that the five-litre keg projects from the kitchen draining board as it disgorges its foaming, lukewarm beer is that of the cosy, old-fashioned neighbourhood bar or dimly remembered booze-ups in the student union.

5 Million Senseo Crema Fans Can't Be Wrong

And now for the Senseo Crema (there, I said it). Ah, that oh so successful coffee-making appliance from Philips, which sold in its millions, first conquering the Netherlands and then the rest of Western Europe; the Senseo Crema, with which the product managers of Philips and Douwe Egberts unerringly zeroed in on a new market of two-income couples and prospective espresso addicts.

Although Dutch industrial design products went conspicuously unmentioned in *False Flat*, the Senseo turned spontaneously into a topic of widespread discussion during the PR tour Betsky held after the appearance of his book. Design engineers from the consumer-market design studios were openly surprised at the absence of the appliance from *False Flat*, and they defended the Philips coffee maker fervently at public meetings and in design journals. They saw the Senseo as a perfect blend of clever engineering, commercial nous, innovation, and marketing. The engineers were all too keen to raise the topic of the new class of appliance which had resulted from their collaboration with the marketeers, and of the smart thinking behind the patented coffee pads which would continue generating income ad infinitum.

Even the latest offshoot of scientific design research added its two cents' worth: the Design and Emotion community used the Senseo to illustrate how consumers appreciate, nay, intensively experience!, a new product. In the footsteps of Raymond Loewy, they had discovered that to be successful a new product had to differ a bit from what was familiar to the average consumer, but not too much; and that recognition did not necessarily have to concern a product of the same type. The Senseo was indeed a new product type, but not so new that it did not convey a gentle hint (ac-

cording to some researchers) of the coffee-waiter's servile bow, or (so thought others) of a slightly half-hearted morning erection.

The fat finally hit the fire, however, when Betsky admitted, in public and in the presence of the coffee machine's designers, to finding the commercially triumphant Senseo an uninteresting product. In his view, it was not typical of original Dutch design and its visual styling was too non-specific. 'Our Yankee friend', wrote an angry reader in a letter to the 'Product' magazine, 'has deliberately skimmed over the technical qualities of the appliance, and, damn it, has said even less about the overwhelming success of the Senseo as a commercial product. The nerve of the guy! Didn't he know how many...'.

Yes, Betsky knew. Some 5 million Senseos had already been sold, and the implicit message of the proponents of the either pale blue or ivory-coloured coffee machine was that the improbable sales figures were the best proof of quality. It was the same argument America's first global rock 'n' roll superstar, Elvis Presley, had offered to in an attempt not only to stress the commercial success of his music but to evade questions about its musical quality. In 1959, the King brought out a collection of his greatest hits on the LP '50 Million Elvis Fans Can't Be Wrong'. A better title could hardly have been chosen. Elvis could feel it in his bones by the late 50s that the furore of the early years was waning. He saw that rising young rock groups from the UK stood ready to become the heart-throbs of the countless teenage girl fans whom he had so expertly enthralled just a few years before. After a salvo of sugary feature films, in retrospect excruciating to

Fig 9.1   5 Million Senseo Crema
Fans Can't be wrong
image: Corrie van der Lelie

watch, Elvis was no longer the pre-eminent rock 'n' roll rebel of his time but had become a crooner on the level of Pat Boone or Paul Anka. This certainly did no harm to the sheer volume of fans or to the contents of his coffers, but was he still exciting and provocative? No, those days had gone.

Forever progressive

Like a Colonel Parker in reverse, Aaron Betsky challenged the important of the Senseo's astonishing commercial success. At the same time he was right, of course, in his assessment of the design of many Dutch industrial products. Anyone entering a Dutch household goods chain store like Blokker will not be delayed by the seductive curves of the Senseo in his hasty progress along the shelves full of cheap plastic electric kettles, mass-produced white porcelain figurines, and gaudy artificial flowers. But can it have been the deprecation of visual quality uttered by an occupant of the cultural elite's ivory tower that invoked the fury of the Dutch business world and the design studios? Not at all, Mr. Betsky: they were crying all the way to the bank. The shoe pinched rather in an entirely different place, namely in Betsky's analysis of the situation. The presence of an essentially nostalgic trait in the modernism of the eighties and nineties identified by Hans van Dijk and the like may well have been widely accepted in the architectural discourse, but scarcely anything of this outlook filtered through to the paper-thin discourse of product design. To many denizens of that world, the encounter with the concept of romantic modernism came as an insult either to

their self-styled avant-garde aspirations or to the innovativeness they ascribed to their own work and ideas. Being a successor to the Bauhaus was, after all, a guarantee for a criticism-proof, life-long career of progressive design, wasn't it? Or so it was held in the design training schools such as the Industrial Design department at Delft University of Technology. The design engineers rightly wondered what role would be left for them if Betsky succeeded in capturing the Dutch design spirit in a paradigm of reality reshuffled and intensified, instead of one of technological innovation and Utopia. They realized all too well that Betsky's characterization was, unfortunately for him but agonizingly for the design engineers, actually perfectly applicable to the Senseo, the Beertender, and the sunray lamp. These products, too, are the result of a reshuffling of part of the real world, respectively the Italian coffee bar, the student pub, and a vacation in the sun. Marketeering circles triumphantly term products like these, which do not embody a technical advance but aspire to a change in user behaviour, 'usage innovations' (bear in mind that, in the absence of real advance, this qualification may equally be applied to the improved styling of a diaper, or for a newly introduced cocktail snack). Besides, it is quite astonishing that the above-mentioned Dutch innovations all relate to a consumer who has seen far more of the world than we ever thought possible in our futuristic years. Perhaps Betsky would claim that it is these international aspirations in particular that are revamped in a typically Dutch way and transposed to the domestic interior. But, if so, he is right again: the Dutch designer seldom creates a springboard to a new world

– recall the diffident Dutch response to the digital anno mirabilis, 2000 – but is a past master at exploiting the new possibilities once they become available.

After this provisional conclusion, we have no choice but to concur with Betsky's final proposal: the establishment of a Dutch 'house of design'. That would be a place where not only the designing disciplines such as architecture, fashion and graphic design come together, but also where Dutch Design, Hema Modernism (the Dutch brand of chain-store modernism) and the scientifically trained design engineers could meet. Perhaps that really would be a Utopia, and, in that Holland House, we could square up to both the well-nigh reactionary nostalgic prejudices of Dutch Design and the invariably run-of-the-mill styling of our usage-innovative products. Considering the prevailing mentality of designers in the Netherlands, it would stand a good chance of being a typically Dutch Utopia.

"The Aula is an extraordinary vivid argument about its times, a mighty concrete diplodocus ... [designed] near the peak of the Cold War. (...) It's hard still to see an optimism in its brutalism, except in the assumption that the fight is worth fighting. In a world of Mutually Assured Destruction – a serious madness – architecture offered a standing, strong animal form – one of us, sheltering us – ennobled by its obvious determination to resist."
— Paul S. Byard, "Using the NAI, A Work in Progress", Architecture Bulletin 01.

Letter to the Editor

The Aula and the Cold War

I began reading the first article of the excellent-looking Architecture Bulletin with pleasurable expectations. And those expectations did not prove unfounded. I must admit I have seldom laughed so heartily over an article about architecture as over Paul Byard's "Using the NAI". I had intriguing visions of Van den Broek and his collaborating architect Jan de Groot working behind locked doors, now and then looking nervously over their shoulders and pessimistically sketching their "launching ramp for an act of defence against a form of evil". Bakema would occasionally bang on the door, which then creaked cautiously open so that he too could make his contribution to the design. And later, during construction, there was a heavily guarded site office in Delft with a triple fence around it – a bit like the American Embassy in The Hague – where the project architects Henk Lops and Gerard Lans and their staff had to show security passes and endure frisking before they were allowed entry to work on their "Star Wars fighter". Incidentally, their "argument about its times", meaning the 1970s, was actually made between 1961 and 1964.

Let me put Paul Byard straight. I can assure him that, in relation to the Aula design, not a single thought about the Cold War has ever arisen among all the people who have worked there. On the contrary, you could even argue that Van den Broek did his best to counteract the Cold War mentality. In that very period he was, as vice-president of the Union Internationale des Architectes, one of those who persisted in pressing for a major congress in Cuba; and it took place, too, complete with a long speech by Fidel Castro and with Che Guevara chairing one day's sessions. I suspect that is something Byard could not even imagine, considering the George Bush-style rhetoric he uses in his article.

On top of that, he is a poor observer or perhaps he did not actually visit the building. He speaks of it as a "dark uncomfortable curiosity" – and that is hard to picture for anyone who is familiar with the building's light, transparent atmosphere and its convincing spatial coherence. Maybe if he had been using his eyes he might not have crashed his bicycle... And isn't it always the case that you see what you want to see, and that your interpretation of what you see is partly shaped by your own (American) upbringing and history? He does not seem to be much of an animal-lover, at least: he describes the Aula as an animal, and says the same for Jean Nouvel's extension to the Rein Sofia Museum in Madrid. I wonder what species of beast he has in mind here? Nor does he hold extinct birds in great esteem, describing the Aula roof as "a dunce-cap that shoots out of the ground as if to dramatize what dodos we are if we don't get thinking". Can you picture it?

Still, I heartily agree with him that the way Mecanoo Architecten designed the library behind the Aula is of exceptional merit.

— Frans Hooykaas (member of the firm Van den Broek & Bakema from 1961-1990).